D1615846

the Art Question

'A very good book. Clear, concise and engaging.'
James Elkins, author of *What Painting Is* and *Pictures and Tears*

'What is art?' is a question many of us want answered but are too afraid to ask. It is the very question that Nigel Warburton demystifies in this brilliant and accessible little book. With the help of varied illustrations, from Cézanne and Francis Bacon, to Warhol and Damien Hirst, Warburton brings a philosopher's eye to the art question in a refreshing, jargon-free style.

The Art Question is a stimulating and handy guide through the art maze and is essential reading for anyone interested in art or philosophy, or for those who simply like looking at and thinking about pictures.

Nigel Warburton is the author of the bestsellers *Philosophy: The Basics* (3rd edition), *Thinking from A to Z* (2nd edition), *Philosophy: The Classics* (2nd edition), *Philosophy: Basic Readings*, and *Freedom: An Introduction with Readings*, all published by Routledge. He is also editor of a book on the photographer Bill Brandt and is writing a biography of the architect Ernö Goldfinger.

the Art Question

by Nigel Warburton

Routledge
Taylor & Francis Group

LONDON AND NEW YORK

First published 2003 by Routledge
2 Park Square, Milton Park, Abingdon, Oxon, OX14 4RN

Simultaneously published in the USA and Canada
by Routledge
270 Madison Avenue, New York, NY 10016

Reprinted 2006, 2007, 2008, 2010

Routledge is an imprint of the Taylor & Francis Group

Typeset in Janson and Neue Helvetica by
Keystroke, Jacaranda Lodge, Wolverhampton
Printed and bound in India by Replika Press Pvt. Ltd.

British Library Cataloguing in Publication Data
A catalogue record for this book is available from the British Library

Library of Congress Cataloging in Publication Data
Warburton, Nigel, 1962-
    The art of question/Nigel Warburton.
    p. cm.
    Includes bibliographical references and index.
    1. Art-Philosophy. I. Title.
    N70 .W37 2002   2002031729

ISBN 978-0-415-17489-3 (hbk)
ISBN 978-0-415-17490-9 (pbk)

For Duncan MacAskill

Contents

		Illustrations	ix
		Acknowledgements	xi
Introduction	ǀ	Art and Philosophy	1
Chapter One	ǀ	Significant Form	9
Chapter Two	ǀ	Expression of Emotion	37
Chapter Three	ǀ	Family Resemblances	65
Chapter Four	ǀ	Institutional Contexts	87
Chapter Five	ǀ	So What?	121
		Notes	135
		Bibliography	139
		Further Reading	143
		Index	145

Illustrations

Introduction	*A Real Work of Art* Mark Wallinger	xii
Chapter One	Detail from *The Railway Station*	
	W. P. Frith	8
	Lac d'Annecy Paul Cézanne	17
	David Hume Allan Ramsay	28
	Regentesses of the Old Men's Alms House	
	Frans Hals	30–1
Chapter Two	*A Pair of Shoes* Vincent Van Gogh	36
	Passport Photos Francis Bacon	44
	Three studies for *Figures at the Base of a*	
	Crucifixion Francis Bacon	45–7
	'Psycho' shower scene Alfred Hitchcock	53
	The Wilton Diptych	58–9
Chapter Three	*The Osmonds*	64
	My Bed Tracey Emin	75

Chapter Four	*Novecento (Twentieth century)*	
	Maurizio Cattelan	86
	The Physical Impossibility of Death in the Mind of Someone Living	
	Damien Hirst	88–9
	Brillo Box Andy Warhol	92
	Storyville, plate 33 E. J. Bellocq	104
	Schooner under the Moon Alfred Wallis	107
Chapter Five	*Tiananmen Square, 4th June, 1989*	
	Stuart Franklin	120
	Untitled Film Still #21 Cindy Sherman	128

Acknowledgements

I am very grateful for comments from Michael Beaney, Michael Clark, Nicola Durbridge, Keith Frankish, Stuart Franklin, Jonathan Hourigan, Joanna Kerr, Stephen Law, Colin Lyas, Duncan MacAskill, Derek Matravers, Stephen Moller, Anna Motz, Alex Orenstein, Sara Parkin and a number of anonymous publishers' readers – some of whose advice I have taken. I also want to thank my agent, Caroline Dawnay, and my editors at Routledge: Adrian Driscoll, Tony Bruce, Muna Khogali and Ruth Bourne. My ideas about the art question have been focused by discussions with the numerous Open University undergraduates I have met at summer schools and as a tutor for AA301 *Philosophy of the Arts*.

Nigel Warburton, 2002

Introduction | Art and Philosophy

The art question is the question 'what is art?' It has been important both in twentieth-century aesthetics and in art practice. At times it has seemed that artists have had to confront it in their work in order to be taken seriously by the art world. As I write this, the Belgian artist Francis Alys has chosen to send a live peacock to the Venice Biennale instead of attending himself. The peacock's activity is presented as a work of art entitled *The Ambassador*. The artist's British dealers have provided a helpful gloss on the meaning of this work of art:

> The bird will strut at all the exhibitions and parties, as if he is the artist himself. It is anecdotal, insinuating the vanity of the art world and tying in old animal fables.[1]

Presumably someone was on hand to clear up this surrogate artist's minor works during the Biennale. Perhaps these will be exhibited at a future Biennale.

A Real Work of Art, Mark Wallinger, Anthony Reynolds Gallery

Alys is by no means the first artist to present a living animal as a work of art. Mark Wallinger's *A Real Work of Art* (see p. xii), for example, is a racehorse and has run in competition. Its name is not intended as metaphor. It is literally a work of art. It is a real racehorse that has raced as well as a real work of art. Naming the horse and advertising its existence is a challenge to most accepted views about what art is. And that, in a sense, is the point – or at least a good part of it. In the creation of artworks like these – a genre dubbed 'anxious objects' by the art critic Harold Rosenberg – artists approach the condition of philosophers. They see their predecessors as implying a theory of art that they neatly refute with a well-chosen counter-example. In time such counter-examples themselves become absorbed into the mainstream and lose their power to shock. They eventually become the targets of a new avant-garde. And so art evolves in strange and unpredictable directions.

The best-known example of such disruptive gestures – which is pivotal in most discussions of the art question – is Marcel Duchamp's *Fountain*. This was a white porcelain urinal daubed with the pseudonym 'R. Mutt' that he submitted in 1917 to the Society for Independent Artists' Exhibition in New York. The exhibition was supposed to be open – contributors had to pay six dollars, for which they could exhibit two works. Duchamp paid the fee, but his work was still rejected. The president of the board of the society declared in a press statement that Duchamp's *Fountain* was 'by no definition, a work of art'.[2] Alfred Stieglitz's photograph of *Fountain* appeared in the second issue of a magazine, *The Blind Man*, together with a discussion of 'The Richard Mutt case' that included the following justification, answering the complaint that this was 'a plain piece of plumbing', not art:

Whether Mr. Mutt with his own hands made the fountain or not has no importance. He CHOSE it. He took an ordinary article of life, placed it so that its useful significance disappeared under the new title and point of view – created a new thought for that object.[3]

So it was a work of art by *some* definition. With *Fountain* and other 'readymades' – a technical term coined by Duchamp – Duchamp challenged confidence about what art could and should be. Whether or not *Fountain* began as a joke, the point Duchamp made through it has become serious with time. The idea that all works of art must be the product of the artist's hand, or that they must be aesthetically beautiful or emotionally profound, is hard to sustain once works like *Fountain* have been accepted into the mainstream, as they have.

As I've suggested, anxious objects like *The Ambassador*, *A Real Work of Art* and *Fountain* provide a kind of visual philosophy that addresses and answers the art question. But to treat them as an adequate substitute for philosophy is a mistake. Most are one-liners. Philosophy has more to say about this question than is possible through a work of visual art. This book, inasmuch as it is a work of philosophy, probably shouldn't end up as an exhibit in an art gallery. Philosophy is a critical engagement with ideas in words. It involves argument and counter-argument, example and counter-example. Philosophers don't just express their beliefs; they justify them with evidence and argument. They reason, they define, they clarify. Above all, they are interested in truth, forever trying to get beyond appearances. They attempt to set out their position with a clarity and rigour that will allow them to be challenged, criticized perhaps. Philosophy, then, is not a matter of manifestos and gestures, but of reasoned cases argued through to conclusions.

It can still be passionate and lively despite this. It needn't be mere logic-chopping.

The art question seems most suited to a philosophical rather than an artistic response. Yet that is not to say that philosophy has any simple answer to it. Indeed, one of the products of studying philosophy is an awareness that most apparently simple questions cannot be answered simply. Philosophy may provide a theoretical underpinning for our most cherished beliefs; but equally it may show us how little we know. The Delphic oracle deemed Socrates the wisest man in Athens, which came as a surprise to him, as he felt that he didn't know anything for certain. But, through his questioning of those who were confident that they knew what they were talking about, Socrates came to realise that the oracle was right. His wisdom lay in knowing the limits of his knowledge, whereas others dogmatically asserted indefensible opinions. My main aim in this book is to lay bare a range of indefensible positions, revealing the counter-arguments and counter-examples that undermine these positions.

In view of the difficulty of saying something both positive and true about art, it can be tempting to dismiss the art question altogether. Why bother philosophising about works of art at all? Barnett Newman suggested that artists need art theory like birds need ornithology. But there *is* a real question here, one worth investigating, precisely because it is so puzzling. And it seems to get more puzzling the more artists challenge the notion of what art is. The question is most obviously posed by anxious objects. Yet, once you've recognised the question, it can be just as intractable when you consider cases of mainstream art. It is certainly worth devoting some energy to attempting to answer the question, or at least to show why it can't be answered.

This book explores several of the major philosophical attempts to answer the art question in the twentieth century. Most of the thinkers I discuss are within what has come to be known as the analytic tradition in philosophy, and all have focused on the visual arts. I have not treated their theories as mummified exhibits in an archaeological museum, but rather as potential contributions to an ongoing debate. They are, of course, intimately tied to the period in which they were written. But that doesn't preclude us learning from insights which may be relevant to our present-day concerns – if this weren't so, it would be hard to justify looking at them at all. All of them have some life in them and some contribution to make.

I begin with Clive Bell's formalist account of art. He argues that all art of all ages has a common denominator – significant form. R. G. Collingwood, the subject of Chapter Two, argued that the common core of art was its peculiar form of emotional expression, the clarifying of what begins as a vague feeling. Chapter Three examines the argument that art has defied definition because it is not the sort of concept that can ever be defined in terms of common denominators. Drawing on Wittgenstein's insights into the nature of language, holders of this view argue that art is a family resemblance term. In Chapter Four, I engage with one of the most important recent theories of art, the Institutional Theory. This leads into a discussion of its descendant, known rather awkwardly as 'defining art historically'. In the final chapter I offer my own hypothesis about the art question, and illustrate it with a comparison of two photographs.

This book is meant for anyone interested in the art question. It does not presuppose any knowledge of philosophy, and little of art. I hope that artists and art-lovers as well as students of philosophy will read it. A great deal of pretentious nonsense has been written about art. I have tried very hard not to add to this nonsense. I have deliberately kept the book short and to the point, not least because I believe that those who are truly interested in visual art should spend a significant part of their lives looking at paintings, drawings, prints, sculptures, photographs and so on, and not just reading about them.

Chapter One | Significant Form

Clive Bell's book *Art*, first published in 1914, is a manifesto as much as a theory about what art is. Its passionate polemic does not disguise the fact that its main purpose was to justify taking Paul Cézanne's painting seriously. The original title of the book was 'The New Renaissance'. For Bell, Cézanne occupied the highest throne in the heaven of Post-Impressionism, much as Michelangelo had in Vasari's progressive account of the Renaissance artists, *The Lives of the Artists*. *Art* was one of the first bombshells in what Bell later dubbed 'The Battle of Post-Impressionism'. Along with Roger Fry, Bell had organised the two great Post-Impressionist exhibitions in London in 1910 and 1912, the effects of which were still reverberating among traditionalists when *Art* was published. Yet Bell's book is more than mere rhetoric in defence of an avant-garde school of art. It contains within it a theory about what visual art is, and a programme for looking at paintings.

Detail from *The Railway Station* (1862), W. P. Frith, courtesy of The Bridgeman Art Library/Royal Holloway and Bedford New College, Surrey, UK

Bell's theory can be summed up in the phrase 'Art is significant form'. This is the main message of the section of the book called 'The aesthetic hypothesis'. The theory is essentially this. Some objects, created by human hands, have, for whatever reason, been charged with a power to produce an aesthetic emotion in sensitive viewers. These objects are all around us, and when we are interested in them as works of art it is irrelevant when they were made, who made them, or why. The power to produce an aesthetic emotion is inherent in significant form. Significant form is a combination of lines, shapes and colours in certain relations. Not all form is *significant* form; but, if an object has significant form, it has it because of the relations between these lines, shapes and colours. This, Bell argued, is 'the one quality common to all works of visual art'. Representation – what a painting is of – is irrelevant to our appreciation of works of art as art. It is not that Bell thinks that there is anything intrinsically wrong with representation; but rather that the *artistic* value of visual art lies elsewhere:

> the representative element in a work of art may or may not be harmful; always it is irrelevant. For, to appreciate a work of art we need bring with us nothing from life, no knowledge of its ideas and affairs, no familiarity with its emotions.[1]

Art, then, isn't about life, even when it seems to be. The only relevant knowledge the viewer need have is a sense of form and colour and of three-dimensional space. This last element is Bell's sole concession to the representational aspects of painting:

> Pictures which would be insignificant if we saw them as flat patterns are profoundly moving because, in fact, we see them as related planes.

> If the representation of three-dimensional space is to be called 'representation', then I agree that there is one kind of representation which is not irrelevant. Also, I agree that along with our feeling for line and colour we must bring with us our knowledge of space if we are to make the most of every kind of form.[2]

Despite suggesting that representation within a painting may not be harmful, he is scornful of what he calls 'descriptive painting'. At their worst, descriptive paintings merely convey information, and if they have an emotional effect on their viewers it is because they suggest emotions rather than act as objects of emotions. This is brought out in his discussion of William Powell Frith's *Paddington Station* (1860–2)[3] (see p. 8), which he declares is not a work of art, but merely 'an interesting and amusing document'. In this painting, which shows a crowded platform at Paddington Station,

> line and colour are used to recount anecdotes, suggest ideas, and indicate the manners and customs of an age: they are not used to provoke aesthetic emotion.[4]

Paddington Station is a conglomeration of little tableaux which are designed to intrigue. For example, the artist has painted himself and his wife and children in a family group saying farewell to a boy who is presumably going off to boarding school; on another part of the platform two well-known London detectives, Michael Haydon and James Brett, are arresting a man about to board the train; and the art dealer, Louis Victor Flatow, who commissioned the picture, is seen talking to the engine driver. The canvas is filled with such interactions. Frith probably painted the scene from a series of photographs, and this contributes to the rather disjointed composition. What the viewer achieves from such a painting is, according to Bell, at best, pleasing distraction brought about by stirring up memories of previously felt emotions. And that, we are told, is not the purpose of art: 'to use art as a means to the emotions of life is to use a telescope for reading the news'. Such a painting could never lead to aesthetic rapture since as a pattern of lines, shapes and colours it is disjointed and unappealing. It lacks significant form.

This might sound as if in talking about significant form Bell is simply describing and celebrating our reactions to beauty. Paintings can be beautiful even if they depict ugly people or events; actual views can be beautiful even though they don't represent anything at all. However, this is not Bell's position. The aesthetic emotion that plays so central a role in his theory is not typically felt in the presence of anything but works of art. He uses 'aesthetic emotion' as a technical term: it does not mean for him just any emotion that we might happen to label aesthetic. The aesthetic emotion is peculiar to our appreciation of art, and in the rare instances in which it is aroused by natural objects this is somehow derivative of its primary meaning. The beauty we recognise and feel when we look at a butterfly's wing or a flower is not, for Bell, of the same kind as the significant form of a painting. Combinations of lines and colours produced by human hands can arouse us to the aesthetic emotion, an emotion that at its height can be ecstatic; natural beauty rarely if ever does this. The emotions that natural beauty arouses are of a different kind. Or at least that is Bell's assertion. In Evelyn Waugh's *Brideshead Revisited*, the narrator, Charles Ryder, is convinced by a counter-assertion:

it was not until Sebastian, idly turning the page of Clive Bell's *Art*, read: "'Does anyone feel the same kind of emotion for a butterfly or a flower that he feels for a cathedral or a picture?' Yes. I do," that my eyes were opened.[5]

For Bell the aesthetic emotion is not an emotion of general life; it is something more profound. In the section of *Art* called 'The metaphysical hypothesis', Bell suggests that the significant form provides us with a glimpse of the structure of the world as it really is, a glimpse behind the veil of appearances. Here he comes very close to Arthur Schopenhauer's belief that works of art, and in particular works of music, could give us insight into the ultimate nature of reality, taking us much deeper than the surface level of mere appearance. Bell offers this metaphysical hypothesis far more tentatively than his aesthetic hypothesis. The core of his theory of art is delivered in his discussion of our experience of significant form rather than in his speculations about its possible causes. Nevertheless, the section on the metaphysical hypothesis is interesting and revealing.

The glimpse of ultimate reality that significant form can give is not achieved directly. It is a consequence of the artist expressing an emotion he or she has felt about some real or imagined aspect of the world. The artist manages to see, for example, a chair as pure form, devoid of associations and function. This gives rise to a deep and inspired emotion. The artist's aesthetic vision of the pure form of the chair is a vision of an object stripped of all everyday concerns. This vision lays bare the object as it is in itself. The artist's emotion towards this vision is then expressed in the painting of the chair.

This hypothesis gives Bell an explanation for his preference for original paintings and drawings over copies or forgeries. He writes: 'A literal copy is seldom reckoned even by its owner a work of art. It leaves us cold; its forms are not significant.'[6] Yet it follows from his theory that if two paintings were identical mark for mark, Bell would have to say that if one had significant form then the other one would necessarily possess it too. Such forms are in principle open to replication, particularly when the painting or drawing in question is relatively uncomplicated. Bell, however, doubts whether such replication ever actually occurs:

> Evidently, it is impossible to imitate a work of art exactly; and the differences between the copy and the original, minute though they may be, exist and are felt immediately.[7]

The copy or forgery lacks something that the original has. The reason Bell gives for his belief in the impossibility of a perfect copy of a work of art is that the original marks on canvas or paper were the effects of a particular state of mind experienced by the artist. The person copying or forging the picture won't have the same state of mind and so won't be able to replicate the lines, shapes and colours perfectly. Good copies, however, are possible. But they aren't *literal* copies. They are achieved when the artist sets aside any attempt to produce an exact copy and instead translates the art of others into his or her own language:

> The power of creating significant form depends, not on hawklike vision, but on some curious mental and emotional power. Even to copy a picture one needs, not to see as a trained observer, but to feel as an artist.[8]

Thus, the artist's emotion may well be what gives significant form the power to produce an aesthetic emotion but, Bell warns, it is the significant form that the viewer should seek, not the expression of emotion: 'It is useless to go to a picture gallery in search of expression; you must go in search of significant form.'[9] Not everyone is fortunate enough to be able to appreciate visual art. Those who cannot do not feel the aesthetic emotion even in the presence of great works. As Bell puts it, 'they are deaf men at a concert'. Such people may know intellectually that they are standing in front of a great painting, but they can never truly feel the effect of significant form. Such a picture is charged with the power to produce the aesthetic emotion, yet without the presence of a sensitive viewer it will lie dormant. Bell suggests that those who are content with 'the smug foothills of warm humanity' – presumably those who prefer Frith's *Paddington Station* to Cézanne's masterpieces – can have no idea of 'the austere and thrilling raptures of those who have climbed the cold, white peaks of art'.

This theory puts art beyond the contingencies of time and place. It makes great art universal:

> Great art remains stable and unobscure because the feelings that it awakens are independent of time and place, because its kingdom is not of this world. To those who have and hold a sense of the significance of form what does it matter whether the forms that move them were created in Paris the day before yesterday or in Babylon fifty centuries ago?[10]

When we respond to art appropriately we respond in the way that sensitive human beings have responded throughout history.

Read as a manifesto for Cézanne and other Post-Impressionist painters, this theory is relatively uncontroversial. It suggests a way of approaching these artists' work which locates them within the great tradition of Western painting. Despite their apparent radical departure towards abstraction, at a deeper level, artists like Cézanne, Matisse and Picasso were simply doing what artists have always done. According to Bell, these artists produced objects with significant form. Bell's theory also suggests a way of approaching what were at the time seen as 'difficult' paintings: don't become weighed down with historical and art-historical information; pay attention to the lines, shapes and colours in front of you; ignore, for the most part, any representational element the paintings might have; and then you will experience them as art – provided, of course, that you are visually sensitive and they have significant form.

To understand the practical implications of Bell's theory of art, consider how he would approach a particular painting. Cézanne's *Lac d'Annecy* (see p. 17), painted in 1896, hangs in the Courtauld Gallery in Somerset House, London. It is a serene image of a château at the foot of some hills seen from across a lake. Forms have been simplified and abstracted, but the subject matter is still recognisable. At the same time this is a vibrant painting dominated by planes of rich blues and gentler greens. In order to appreciate a picture such as this, according to Bell, we need to look at its forms, setting aside the associations of the depicted landscape or the background knowledge that we have of the painter's life. The painting, we shall assume, has significant form, and that is the cause of the exquisite emotion it stirs within the breast of sensitive viewers. This emotion is very different from anything they might feel in front of the landscape itself. Cézanne's simplification of

Lac d'Annecy (1896), Paul Cézanne, courtesy of the Courtauld Institute Gallery, Somerset House, London

forms is an instantiation of the Post-Impressionist creed spelt out by Bell: 'Every sacrifice made to representation is something stolen from art'.[11]

Such a painting illustrates Bell's theory well since in it Cézanne manipulated the relations between the parts of the composition for the sake of form, and had little concern for literal accuracy. In reality, for instance, the château is a mile away across the lake from Cézanne's viewpoint, and would have appeared tiny in a photograph of the scene. In the painting it dominates. Similarly, the background hillsides have been stylised to give a more symmetrical relationship of forms than would have been visible at the scene. Here Cézanne is consciously producing 'a harmony parallel to nature'.[12] He is not attempting to hold a mirror up to nature. Rather he is producing a pattern that parallels the visual experience of the scene and also expresses the artist's emotional reaction to it. The actual landscape only provides the 'aesthetic problem' to which the painting is the solution. The *real* concern, however, is with form. And this, too, should be the viewer's concern. Looking at this painting can give rise to a profound aesthetic emotion and perhaps even transport us beyond the everyday world of mere appearance that we ordinarily inhabit.

Bell produced his theory by working back from his experience of paintings such as *Lac d'Annecy*. He realised that in this sort of painting it was form, colour and design that moved him rather than subject matter, and then generalised from such a case to all art. Like most philosophical theories about the nature of art, Bell's was a reaction to a contemporary movement in art rather than a catalyst for such a movement.

If we are to treat Bell's theory as more than a manifesto and take seriously its claims to answer the question 'what is art?', then it will have to meet some quite serious objections. Some of those objections arise from its intuitionist tendency. Though not a professional philosopher, Bell, like many other members of the Bloomsbury set, was deeply influenced by the Cambridge philosopher G. E. Moore. Moore, in his book *Principia Ethica* (1903), which Bell cites approvingly, had argued that 'good', when used in a moral sense, was indefinable. It could not be resolved into smaller constituent parts. The way that we distinguish good actions from bad or evil ones is by intuition – hence the tag 'intuitionism'. Any theory which attempted to explain in a general way what made an action morally good or bad was dismissed as committing the 'naturalistic fallacy'. This is the alleged mistake of attempting to derive value judgements from facts alone. If, for example, someone declared that a particular action, such as giving money to charity, was morally good *because* it maximised happiness (a utilitarian justification), Moore would point out that this was a *non sequitur*. Once you had demonstrated that an action maximised happiness, it would still be an open question as to whether or not it was a morally good action. No description of facts could, for Moore, entail an evaluative conclusion. This was a logical point. Moore argued that we cannot deduce evaluative conclusions from factual descriptions, but must rather simply recognise the moral goodness of certain kinds of action.

Moore's intuitionism in ethics cast its influence upon a whole generation of British intellectuals. In many ways, Bell's theory of significant form mirrors its structure. The sensitive critic knows when he or she is in the presence of significant form by means of the equivalent of an intuition, namely an episode of the aesthetic emotion. This aesthetic emotion cannot be broken down into smaller constituent parts. It is simply the emotion that is felt in the presence of works of art. Similarly, significant form cannot be explained in terms of its parts. Sensitive people can just recognise these things. Anyone who tried to deduce the aesthetic worth of a painting merely from a description of its objective observable features would be guilty of a logical mistake. Describe any feature of an artwork and it will still remain an open question as to whether or not it is a good work of art, and, indeed, whether it is a work of art at all.

In an influential passage of *Principia Ethica*, Moore concluded that by far the most valuable things in life are states of consciousness, and in particular 'the pleasures of human intercourse and the enjoyment of beautiful objects'. This view provided Bell with the underpinning for one of his more extravagant claims, namely that 'there are no qualities of greater moral value than artistic qualities'. For Bell, art had moral worth because it was the best means to the highest states of consciousness, namely those of aesthetic contemplation. His writing, consequently, often has an almost evangelical tone. Art might be autonomous – a separate realm – but it was through art that humanity achieved its most refined and important experiences.

Yet from a distance of almost ninety years it is hard to see how either Moore's or Bell's theories came to be taken so seriously. From this perspective Moore's declaration about the good things in life, or Bell's on the moral status of aesthetic evaluation, seem little more than the elevation of individual taste into an objective ideal; supreme acts of will or involuntary autobiography, depending on your position. What may have been acceptable to the Bloomsbury intelligentsia in the first part of the twentieth century does not necessarily hold for all times and in all places.

Some of Bell's assumptions and prejudices emerge in a pivotal paragraph in 'The aesthetic hypothesis':

> For either all works of visual art have some common quality, or when we speak of "works of art" we gibber. . . . There must be some one quality without which a work of art cannot exist; possessing which, in the least degree, no work is altogether worthless. What is this quality? What quality is shared by all objects that provoke our aesthetic emotions? What quality is common to Sta. Sophia and the windows at Chartres, Mexican sculpture, a Persian bowl, Chinese carpets, Giotto's fresco at Padua and the masterpieces of Poussin, Piero della Francesca, and Cézanne? Only one answer seems possible – significant form. In each, lines and colours combined in a particular way, certain forms and relations of forms, stir our aesthetic emotions.[13]

The first sentence of this quotation suggests a dichotomy. All works of visual art must have something in common, or else we end up talking nonsense, gibberish. Yet it is clear that Bell does not believe that when we talk about art we are just making meaningless noises. Consequently he believes all works of art must have some common quality. This, as we shall see in Chapter Three, is not as uncontroversial as it sounds. Bell assumes that if we use a word meaningfully, then there must be a common essence to all the instances of this word. But, setting that aside, consider his claim to have found a common denominator.

The list of objects that Bell takes for granted to be works of art, and which must therefore have something in common, is controversial in several ways. And this is not an accident. It is a piece of rhetoric. He begins with a work of architecture, moves on to an element of architecture, namely the windows of Chartres, but then, after these specific references, interposes Mexican sculpture, a Persian bowl and Chinese carpets as obvious instances of art. Clearly he does not mean all Mexican sculpture or all Persian bowls any more than he means all Chinese carpets, rush mats included. Presumably what he is alluding to are the finest examples of each of these. But, particularly with the examples of bowls and carpets, he is deliberately dissolving any distinction between art and craft. He is making a point here, one which follows from his view that the intended function of objects is irrelevant to our assessment of them as works of art. To include a bowl in a list of allegedly uncontroversial works of art deliberately begs the question on the art/craft distinction. Then to mention Giotto and the masterpieces of Poussin and Piero della Francesca is certainly uncontroversial: but to top this list with 'the *masterpieces* . . . of *Cézanne*' would have baited his more conservative readers in the way that ending such a list with 'the *masterpieces* of Damien Hirst' might today. It is worth remembering in this context that even the distinguished artist John Singer Sargent had described Cézanne as a 'botcher' following the first London Post-Impressionist exhibition and that opinion was deeply divided on the worth of his art. But, even if we concede that all the objects in Bell's list are uncontroversially works of art, is it really true that there can only be one possible common denominator shared by them all? For Bell there was no question: significant form was the only candidate. And significant form gave rise to the aesthetic emotion.

One of the most serious charges levelled at Bell's theory is that it is viciously circular. The alleged circularity occurs in the definition of the two key terms: 'significant form' and 'aesthetic emotion'. The one is defined purely in terms of the other. No further elements are introduced into the circle, and so we have a highly uninformative theory based upon two mutually defined technical terms. There is nothing intrinsically wrong with circularity in argument and definition. Think of a good dictionary: every word defined in that dictionary will be defined in words which are also defined in that dictionary, and so at some level the whole dictionary is circular. Thus, if you were to look up 'cat' and find the definition 'a feline quadruped', then you might look up 'feline' and 'quadruped'. After a series of such moves you would eventually find that every word you had looked up had been defined in terms of other words that you had also looked up. That kind of circularity is completely acceptable. What is unacceptable is the sort of circularity which defines one term *purely* in terms of the other and vice versa. So, for example, if you looked up 'yes' and the definition given was 'the opposite of no'; and then, if you looked up 'no' and the definition given was 'the opposite of yes', you would have good reason for feeling aggrieved. Only if you had some independent way of understanding one of the key terms would you be able to make much sense of this definition. Applying this to Bell's theory of art, we find that significant form is given some explanation: it is a pattern of lines, shapes and colours. However, since this only serves to identify form and not *significant* form, it does not get us much further towards a satisfactory account of art. Significant form is most fully defined as that which gives rise to an aesthetic emotion. This we find is simply the emotion felt in the presence of significant form. Bell does suggest that this emotion can be ecstatic or rapturous, and different from the emotion arising from appreciation of beauty in nature, but this will not serve to distinguish it from numerous other emotions which are not aesthetic in his sense of the word. And he does allow that it need not always reach such heights; so that is of little help. Again, our only real indicator of what an aesthetic emotion is can be found in terms of the other key term of the theory, namely significant form. Hence Bell's theory is viciously circular.

Bell *could*, however, have avoided this problem by giving a more expansive definition of either 'significant form' or 'aesthetic emotion'. If he had given us some independent way of understanding either of these important concepts, then this would have provided a route out of the circle. In the absence of such helpful guides, the fact remains that Bell's theory, when treated as a theory rather than as a manifesto, is, at its heart, devoid of content.

Even if the charge of circularity could be answered, there would still remain some quite serious difficulties with Bell's approach. One practical consequence of the theory as expressed is the fact that there is no obvious method for deciding between competing claims about works of art. For instance, I might claim that Howard Hodgkin's paintings quite obviously manifest significant form. Someone else might reply that they quite clearly don't, that they are crude smudges of garish paint devoid of any important formal qualities. Furthermore, we may both be completely sincere. According to Bell's theory, however, one of us must be right and the other wrong. It can't be true that these objects – Hodgkin's paintings – stand charged with the capacity to evoke an aesthetic emotion and simultaneously do not have this capacity. That would be a direct contradiction, and it would be absurd to embrace it. Yet Bell provides no way of discriminating between these competing claims, and no accreditation process for the sensitive critic. Where there is no consensus amongst apparently sensitive critics, Bell's theory leaves the uncommitted in a quandary.

A further charge that can be levelled at Bell's theory of art is that it is elitist. Bell, presumably, would not see this as an objection to his theory, but rather as a neutral description of its content. Those who do not feel the sort of emotion Bell feels before great works of art are dismissed as 'deaf men at a concert'. To mitigate the effect of this pronouncement Bell confesses that he finds musical form 'exceedingly difficult to apprehend'. This confession is supposed to make the point that receptivity to significant form in the various arts is not evenly distributed. Bell believes that only the fortunate few can make the relevant sorts of discrimination about visual art. So in this sense his theory *is* elitist. In another sense, however, it is not. Traditionally, art historians have demanded that those who would learn about art need first to learn about art history and art theory. This might involve years of studying, often in foreign languages: an option only available to a privileged minority. For Bell, none of this is necessary. You do not need to have attended courses at the Courtauld or the Warburg, nor to have learned Italian in order to appreciate Renaissance art. All you need is a sensitive eye.

Perhaps one reason why Bell is so frequently charged with elitism is that he clearly believed that he and his friends could discern significant form and that those who disagreed with his artistic judgements could not. The charge of elitism doesn't necessarily undermine the theory. It could just be true that ability to discriminate significant form is not widely found. Nevertheless, from a distance, a more plausible hypothesis is that Bell was simply elevating the particular tastes of a small yet influential sub-class of English society into an apparently objective ideal.

D. H. Lawrence, himself a painter as well as a novelist, lampooned the quasi-religiosity of the formalists' message:

> They discovered once more that the aesthetic experience was an ecstasy, an ecstasy granted only to the chosen few, the elect, among

whom said critics were, of course, the arch-elect. This was outdoing Ruskin. It was almost Calvin come to art. But let scoffers scoff, the aesthetic ecstasy was vouchsafed only to the few, the elect, and even then only when they had freed their minds of false doctrines. They had renounced the mammon of 'subject' in pictures, they went whoring no more after the Babylon of painted 'interest', nor did they hanker after the flesh-pots of artistic 'representation'. Oh, purify yourselves, ye who would know the aesthetic ecstasy, and be lifted up to the 'white peaks of artistic inspiration'. Purify yourselves of all base hankering for a tale that is told, and of all low lust for likenesses. Purify yourselves, and know the one supreme way, the way of Significant Form. I am the revelation and the way! I am Significant Form, and my unutterable name is Reality. Lo, I am Form, and I am Pure, behold, I am Pure Form. I am the revelation of Spiritual Life, moving behind the veil. I come forth and make myself known, and I am Pure Form, behold I am Significant Form. . . . Lift up your eyes to Significant Form, and be saved.[14]

Perhaps the most striking feature of Bell's theory is its dismissal of representational aspects of visual art. This was one target of Lawrence's attack in the essay already quoted. For Lawrence, Cézanne, the darling of the formalists, at his best achieved greatness precisely because he *was* interested in representation: 'Cézanne was a realist, and he wanted to be true to life. But he would not be content with the optical cliché.'[15] For Lawrence, the success of Cézanne's still lifes was a success of representation:

Here Cézanne did what he wanted to do: he made the things quite real, he didn't deliberately leave anything out, and yet he gave us a triumphant and rich intuitive vision of a few apples and kitchen pots.[16]

For Bell, in contrast, it was Cézanne's move away from representation in the direction of pure form that made him great.

All traditional theories of visual art have placed a great emphasis on representation. Plato's whole account of what art is was based on the assumption that art imitates nature (which is itself an imitation of the Forms). Art is imitation or *mimesis*. Yet for Bell art had nothing intrinsically to do with representation. If representation occurs, that is incidental to it. What this means in practice is that what a portraitist such as Alan Ramsay was doing when he painted the philosopher David Hume (see p. 28) – and attempted to capture something of the distinctive physiognomy and thus the character of this great philosopher – was only incidental to the creation of the work of art. Bell suggests that we can fully appreciate such a portrait as a work of art, while setting aside any consideration of the fact that it is a portrait of a man who once lived and that it captures something of this man's appearance. It is surely true that portraitists do far more than paint appearances. Formal aspects of paintings can be central, and are rarely irrelevant to our appreciation of those works of art. However, to dismiss all representational elements of paintings as of no concern to the art appreciator is simply implausible.

To be fair to Bell, he does allow representation to serve a function in the production of some pictures. Artists, he tells us, work in response to specific artistic problems that they set themselves. Without an artistic problem to focus on, an artist is likely to dissipate his or her energy. So, for example, a portraitist might set him- or herself the task of producing a psychologically accurate portrait of a sitter. By working within the confines of the conventions of realistic portraiture, this artist might thereby concentrate his or her energy and produce a work which has

significant form. The representational elements do not give the picture significant form, and the picture could have possessed the power to evoke an aesthetic emotion even if it had been purely abstract. But representation is important in so far as it sets the artistic problem to which the painting is the solution.

In some cases, the representational element is so central to a painting that to marginalise it as simply the pretext for formal pattern-making would be absurd. John Berger makes this point in his discussion of a formalist art critic's analysis of *Regentesses of the Old Men's Alms House* by Frans Hals, a group portrait of the Regentesses in charge of a house for old paupers (see pp. 30–1). At the time he painted the portrait (*c.*1664), Hals was old and destitute. The critic concentrates on the compositional unity:

> Each woman stands out with equal clarity against the *enormous* dark surface, yet they are linked by a firm rhythmical arrangement and the subdued diagonal pattern formed by their heads and hands.[17]

Berger concedes that compositional unity contributes to the power of the image. Yet to treat it as though it were itself the emotional charge of the painting is a form of mystification. The formalist terms the critic uses 'transfer the emotion provoked by the image from the plane of lived experience, to that of disinterested "art appreciation". All conflict disappears.'[18] Berger describes the real relationship between the women Hals has been commissioned to portray and the artist. They stare at Hals, 'a destitute old painter who has lost his reputation and lives off public charity'. Yet, as Berger points out:

David Hume (1766), Allan Ramsay, © Trustees of the National Galleries of Scotland 1992/courtesy of the Scottish National Portrait Gallery, Edinburgh

he examines them through the eyes of a pauper who must nevertheless attempt to be objective, i.e., must try to surmount the way he sees as a pauper.[19]

To ignore this element of the painting in favour of attending to formal qualities is perverse. The inadequacies of a purely formalist approach to portraiture are well exposed in this discussion. Formalism just doesn't capture what makes Hals such a great artist. The success of this painting arises in part from the struggle between objective representation and subjective involvement with the sitters and their attitude to the artist.

What becomes apparent in Berger's discussion of the Hals painting is the relevance of context to the understanding of some paintings. Bell was content to treat works of art as independent of the contexts in which they were made and presented. In fact, it should be easier to understand works of art as art, according to Bell's theory, if they are removed from their context or if we know nothing about it. This would allow us to concentrate on the formal aspects, setting aside psychological distractions. But this is implausible. Quite apart from the difficulty of ridding one's mind of the associations that one might have with a particular painting, and a particular subject matter, the act of decontextualising art works either literally or metaphorically is an obstacle to our understanding rather than an aid. It may serve to train the eye, but art appreciation must get beyond the simplistic notion that seeing is innocent.

The objections that Bell ought to have considered representational elements of paintings, and that his theory is too radical in

Regentesses of the Old Men's Alms House (1664), Frans Hals, © The Frans Hals Museum, Haarlem

its decontextualisation of works, are both inconclusive. Bell could simply claim to have different intuitions on the matter. To understand the force of the objections, it is necessary to digress a little. As so often with philosophical objections to theories of art, what is at stake is a balance between pre-existing intuitions (or prejudices in some cases) and general principles. If someone presents a theory of art which runs completely counter to your existing views about particular works of art and their central features, then you will not be likely to accept it. The grounds for accepting it would be if the general principles could be justified. But even then you might still cling to your intuitions as being more certain than the general principles. What usually occurs in such cases is that a compromise is struck. You might make fine adjustments to the general principles in order to meet the counter-examples suggested by your pre-reflective views; or else you might make fine adjustments to your particular judgements in the light of the general principles. This delicate manoeuvring between general principles and particular judgements occurs in a wide range of philosophical situations, and has been given the name 'reflective equilibrium' by the political philosopher John Rawls.[20] Put in these terms, the claim that Bell's theory pays too little attention to representation can be seen as a clash between the general principles of Bell's definition of art and the specific judgements about the relevance of representation that the objector is inclined to make. Similarly, Bell's general principles about art and its eternal qualities come into conflict with many people's intuitions about the relevance of context to understanding particular works of art. In both cases there may be no room for negotiation. Bell would presumably simply respond to this point by declaring that art just *is* significant form, and anyone who denies this is simply mistaken. Representation *is* irrelevant to art. Context *does not* provide a way of understanding art as art. However, given the vicious circularity within his theory, we do not have good grounds for jettisoning what at least at first glance seem to be quite reasonable assumptions about the relevance of representation and context to our understanding of works of art.

Bell's theory is an *aesthetic* one. It concentrates exclusively on visual aspects of works of art: artists' intentions, the historical background, and so on, are irrelevant. What makes something a work of art is its capacity to produce a certain kind of effect in the sensitive appreciator by virtue of its appearance. This sort of theory had more plausibility when Bell was writing at the beginning of the twentieth century. It seems unlikely now to capture in its definition all that we would want to call art. Artists such as Marcel Duchamp, Andy Warhol and Josef Beuys have deliberately produced objects that do not exhibit aesthetic properties as conventionally understood, which nevertheless have been treated as paradigm works of modern art. For all three artists, conceptual aspects of their work can be at least as important as their visual appearance. To understand such works involves an understanding of art theory and of the particular ideas alluded to within the works.

Duchamp's *Fountain* mentioned in the Introduction – a factory-produced urinal which the arist signed and entered for an open art exhibition – challenged conventional notions of what art is. At the time, Bell might quite easily have dismissed it as obviously not a work of art since it did not have significant form. Yet, since such works have gained widespread acceptability, it has become increasingly difficult simply to categorise them as non-art. Historians of art have found no difficulty in accepting that some works of art are self-consciously non-aesthetic, or even anti-aesthetic, in the sense that Bell uses the word 'aesthetic'. Anyone who wants to present a purely aesthetic account of what art is today will be faced with the difficulty of how to cope with works such as Duchamp's *Fountain*. In recent years, philosophers attempting to define art in terms of a common essence, have, with a few exceptions, completely abandoned purely aesthetic accounts. Those who have tried to defend aesthetic theories of art seem curiously out of touch with the post-Dada artistic movements of the twentieth century. Their theoretical accounts read more like nostalgia for a time when aesthetic considerations were central to all works of art, rather than as definitions of what art is now.

One possible diagnosis of where Bell went wrong in *Art* is that he attempted to give a definition of art at all. Bell's is very much a traditional approach to the art question: his answer purports to give necessary and sufficient conditions for something being a work of art. For Bell it is a necessary condition (i.e., a prerequisite) that it be produced by a human being, rather than be a naturally occurring object. And it is both a necessary and sufficient condition that it has significant form. Having significant form, then, is a *prerequisite* which *guarantees* that anything which has it is a work of art. What Bell was trying to do was to discover the common quality shared by all works of art. He did not for one moment doubt that there was such a common quality. However, as we shall see in Chapter Three, there can be grounds for doubting this. Before considering this view, though, I want to examine a different attempt to define art, this time as the expression of emotion.

Chapter Two | Expression of Emotion

> The artist proper is a person who, grappling with the problem of
> expressing a certain emotion, says, "I want to get this clear."[1]

For Bell, as we have seen, 'great art remains stable and unobscure
because the feelings that it wakens are independent of time and
place'.[2] Art is, always has been, always will be Significant Form.
Tempting as it may be to make such an assumption, it is surely
wishful thinking to suppose, as Bell did, that a satisfactory answer
to the question 'what is art now?' will also be a satisfactory
answer to the question 'what *has* art been?' and 'what will it be?' Art
is not a timeless category, but one which evolves as the societies
in which works of art are created evolve.[3]

The Oxford philosopher R. G. Collingwood did not share Bell's
views about the timelessness of art. In the preface to his major work
on the subject, *The Principles of Art* (first published in 1938), he wrote:

I do not think of aesthetic theory as an attempt to investigate and expound eternal verities concerning the nature of an eternal object called Art, but as an attempt to reach, by thinking, the solution of certain problems arising out of the situation in which artists find themselves here and now.[4]

'Here and now' for Collingwood meant England in the 1930s, and the artists whose work most impressed him included Cézanne and T. S. Eliot. Collingwood, however, was not just a philosopher and an enthusiast for the arts. He made a serious study of Romano-British archaeology, publishing important work in the area. His familiarity with Roman artifacts and awareness of their original cultural significance no doubt made him wary of the sort of sweeping generalisation about works of art from other cultures and times which came so easily to Bell. Collingwood, like Bell, had practical experience of painting, a source perhaps of his perceptive analysis of creative processes: both of his parents were artists – his father, William Collingwood (1819–1903), was a well-known English watercolourist and was also for a time secretary to Ruskin. As a child, R. G. Collingwood sketched and painted extensively. In his *Autobiography*, he describes the early experiences which shaped his philosophy of art:

I was constantly watching the work of my father and mother, and the other professional painters who frequented their home, and constantly trying to imitate them; so that I learnt to think of a picture not as a finished product exposed for the admiration of virtuosi, but as the visible record, lying about the house, of an attempt to solve a definite problem in painting, so far as the attempt has gone. I learnt what some critics and aestheticians never know to the end of their lives, that no 'work of art' is ever finished, so that in that sense of the phrase there is no 'work of art' at all. Work ceases upon the picture or manuscript, not because it is finished, but because sending-in day is at hand, or because the printer is clamorous for copy.[5]

Collingwood sees the art question as central to *The Principles of Art*, a book recently described as 'The most influential and readable work in aesthetics in English'.[6] The first line of the introduction makes his focus clear: 'the business of this book is to answer the question: What is art?'[7] Some things labelled art are only 'art falsely so-called' not art proper, a view which Bell would have endorsed. But Collingwood gives a more complicated and systematic analysis of the kinds of thing which are naïvely called art and of what it is that makes works of art proper so very different from them. Most famously, he distinguished art proper from craft. Put simply, craft is an activity which transforms some raw material into a preconceived product following a pre-existent plan. He outlined the cluster of features particularly associated with craft. Craft, for example, involves a distinction between the things used and the result aimed at by using them: the distinction between means and end. So, for instance, a carpenter might use some pieces of wood as the means to produce the end result: a table. Craft also involved a distinction between the plan and its execution. As Collingwood puts it:

> the craftsman knows what he wants to make before he makes it. This foreknowledge is absolutely indispensable to craft: if something, for example stainless steel, is made without such foreknowledge, the making of it is not a case of craft but an accident. Moreover, this foreknowledge is not vague but precise. If a person sets out to make

> a table, and conceives the table only vaguely, as somewhere between
> 2 by 4 feet and 3 by 6, he isn't a craftsman.[8]

Raw material and finished product can be clearly distinguished. The raw material is transformed into something different. The carpenter takes the bits of wood as raw material and out of them makes the finished product, the table. These are some of the most important features of craft that Collingwood isolates. He is not here trying to *define* craft, rather only to suggest the features typical of craft activity. Some of these features may be shared by some works of art, but need not be, since, as we shall see, Collingwood believed that a work of art can exist independently of any physical instantiation of it.

The theory Collingwood labels the technical theory of art, a theory he opposes, recognises no distinction between art and craft. On that theory, art simply is another kind of craft. An artist's task is then one of transforming some raw material into the kind of object which will produce a particular specified effect. He or she is then on a par with anyone who makes things. A blacksmith sets out to make a horseshoe which will fit a particular horse; he or she cuts some iron (the raw material), shapes it at the forge, fits the shoe. The blacksmith knows what the end result should be before the work begins: a well-shod horse. According to the technical theory, an artist goes through analogous stages of selecting materials and shaping them to produce a desired and pre-planned effect.

Collingwood rejects the technical theory of art on the grounds that an artist's activity need not involve a distinction between means and ends. Nor need it involve a distinction between planning and execution. Obviously some works of art do involve planning, particularly those produced as a result of a detailed commission, for example. Anyone who thinks that Michelangelo simply set to with brush and paint when he decorated the ceiling of the Sistine Chapel is naïve. Michelangelo's work involved a great deal of planning. Planning, however, is not a necessary feature of making art, nor distinctive of it. To take Collingwood's example, a sculptor playing with a piece of clay, finding his fingers turning it into a little dancing man, may still have produced a work of art. The fact that he didn't plan to produce such a sculpture, nor knew how it would turn out until he had gone some way towards making it, does not prevent its being a work of art. This is clear from, for instance, the working methods of Picasso, who declared: 'I don't know in advance what I am going to put on the canvas any more than I decide in advance what colours to use.'[9] This undermines the technical theory as an all-encompassing account of art. However, Collingwood goes on to point to further difficulties such as that of specifying the raw material for a work of art. Is the raw material for a poem simply words? Or is it perhaps an emotion? Collingwood's conclusion is that the technical theory of art as a kind of craft is a non-starter. Although works of art may involve craft, art is not to be identified with craft. This is because art is not just a matter of technique; it is not something that can be taught as a skill can be taught: 'a technician is made, but an artist is born'.[10]

One possible target for Collingwood's discussion of the technical theory of art was the Arts and Crafts movement. William Morris, for example, under the influence of Ruskin, greatly admired the works produced by medieval craftsmen. He defined art as 'the expression by man of his pleasure in labour'.[11] Rejecting the celebration of artistic inspiration and artistic genius typical of his time, Morris declared that 'talk of inspiration is sheer nonsense . . . there is no such thing: it is a mere matter of craftsmanship'.[12]

In the same vein, Morris's disciple Walter Crane asserted that 'the true root and basis of all Art lies in the handicrafts'.[13] For Morris and Crane, the celebration of artistic inspiration and the differentiation of art and craft was a distortion of the nature of art.

In contrast, Collingwood presents an essentially romantic view of the artist. He does not, however, go so far as to embrace the sentimental position that anyone at all can produce art (though he does, nevertheless, suggest that those who appreciate art do so by becoming artists themselves). Nor does he anywhere suggest that artists need not learn craft. On the contrary, he believes a certain minimum level of skill is a prerequisite for anyone producing even a modest work of art:

> Great artistic powers may produce fine works of art even though technique is defective; and even the most finished techniques will not produce the finest sort of work in their absence; but all the same, no work of art whatever can be produced without some degree of technical skill, and other things being equal, the better the technique the better will be the work of art. The greatest artistic powers, for their due and proper display, demand a technique as good in its kind as they are in their own.[14]

This last point is worth labouring since Collingwood's views on this matter are often misrepresented. For example, in her book *Aesthetics*, Anne Sheppard takes Collingwood to task because he fails to recognise that 'art may not be all craft but craft plays a considerable part in it'.[15] Collingwood's emphasis in his book is on the expression of emotion. Sheppard's criticism is that this leads him to fail to appreciate the role of craft in art: 'to appreciate Catullus' poetry to the full, one needs to recognise his technical skill as well as respond to the emotions he is expressing'.[16] Yet nothing in Collingwood's theory precludes this sort of response. He says explicitly that the planning characteristic of craft can also be present in works of art: 'if unplanned works of art are possible, it does not follow that no planned work is a work of art'.[17] Indeed, he further speculates:

> it may very well be true that the only works of art which can be made altogether without a plan are trifling ones, and that the greatest and most serious ones always contain an element of planning and therefore an element of craft.[18]

This last quotation also pre-empts a similar criticism made by Robert Wilkinson in his essay 'Art, emotion and expression', where he lists all the six properties of craft identified by Collingwood and then states: 'Collingwood denies that any of these six properties can be predicated of art proper'.[19] He goes on to claim that Collingwood is

> committed to denying that an artist can distinguish between the goal (or end) and the means used to achieve it; or that the execution of the plan of the work of art can be distinguished from the plan itself.[20]

Such misleading interpretations of Collingwood's views on the relationship between art and craft are widespread. And, to be fair to Sheppard and Wilkinson, they arise partly from Collingwood's lack of clarity at key points in *The Principles of Art*. However, Collingwood does emphasise that in at least some cases the production of a work of art need not involve the sorts of conscious planning typical of craft:

The craftsman's skill is his knowledge of the means necessary to realise a given end, and his mastery of those means. A joiner making a table shows his skill by knowing what materials and what tools are need to make it, and being able to use these in such a way as to produce the table exactly as specified.[21]

Creating a work of art is not always like this. It is a mistake to approach artistic creation, as the technical theory does, as if it were necessarily 'The conscious working-out of means to the achievement of a conscious purpose, or in other words technique'.[22]

This recognition of the part played by unconscious, or perhaps pre-conscious, elements, and the relatively minor role that conscious planning may play in the making of a work of art fits well with the way many artists have described the creative act. The painter Francis Bacon, for example, in an interview with David Sylvester, clarified the relationship between what he calls 'intention' and 'surprise':

Passport Photos (c.1960s), Francis Bacon, © Hugh Lane Municipal Gallery of Modern Art, Dublin, and Estate of Francis Bacon

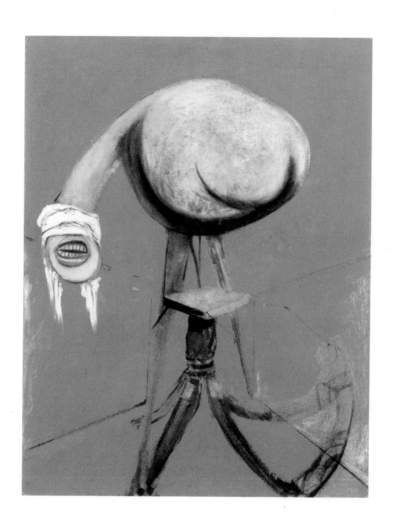

DS   Now, it's clear that in any art there's a mixture of intention and what takes the artist by surprise.

FB   Yes. Without the intention, he's not going to start at all.

DS   What you seem to say is that in your own case surprise takes over from intention quite early on.

FB   You see, one has an intention, but what really happens comes about in working – that's the reason it's so hard to talk about it – it actually does come about in the working. And the way it works is really by the things that happen. In working you are really following this kind of cloud of sensation in yourself, but you don't know what it really is. And it's called instinct. And one's instinct, whether right or wrong, fixes on certain things that have happened in the activity of applying the paint to the canvas.[23]

Bacon goes on to identify conscious self-criticism as another important element in the creative process, but his emphasis is on the unplanned and unconscious contributions to the process. Like Collingwood, Bacon is unwilling to explain the artistic process as fulfilling a clearly formulated intention. The sculptor Ana Maria Pacheco's comments about her approach to woodcarving are similarly in line with Collingwood's distinction between art and craft:

I know of course the structure of the composition, but how it's going to evolve, I don't know. That's why I don't make models, because

Three studies for *Figures at the Base of a Crucifixion* (c.1944), Francis Bacon, courtesy of Tate, London 2001

otherwise it would just be a design. You'd be dealing with what you know. In the visual arts you have to deal with what you don't know.[24]

For both Bacon and Pacheco, it is the process itself which clarifies the initially vague intention. As Collingwood puts it: 'The artist proper is a person who, grappling with the problem of expressing a certain emotion, says, "I want to get this clear."'[25] There is an element of designing while making, of reacting to chance – or, at least, not consciously chosen – marks. And, while some level of skill is needed, skill alone is not sufficient to make a canvas a work of art proper.

The question remains, though, precisely what does Collingwood take art proper to be? It is clear that it is not craft, not the product of techniques used to achieve preconceived ends, or at least it is not essentially this. His answer is simple: art proper is the imaginative expression of emotion. He means something quite specific by 'expression' – not an outpouring or betrayal of emotion, nor a deliberate arousing of emotion, but rather a clarification of an initially vague feeling that through its expression becomes clear. The process of making a work of art is one of refinement of this emotion and at the same time a way for the artist to gain a kind of self-knowledge through clarifying precisely what it is he or she feels:

> Until a man has expressed his emotion, he does not yet know what emotion it is. The act of expressing it is therefore an exploration of his own emotions. He is trying to find out what these emotions are.[26]

This might sound implausible: how could you, for example, be unaware that you were feeling sad? However, on Collingwood's account, the process of exploring the nature of the emotion involves moving from a very general awareness of sadness to a precise imaginative understanding and expression of the unique kind of sadness that the artist is feeling:

> When a man is said to express emotion, what is being said about him comes to this. At first, he is conscious of having an emotion, but not conscious of what that emotion is. All he is conscious of is a perturbation or excitement, which he feels going on within him, but of whose nature he is ignorant. While in this state, all he can say about his emotion is "I feel . . . I don't know what I feel."[27]

The successful expression of an emotion allows the viewer or audience to become conscious of that emotion just as the process of artistic creation focuses the nature of the particular emotion for the person experiencing and expressing it:

> A person who expresses something thereby becomes conscious of what it is that he is expressing, and enables others to become conscious of it in himself and in them.[28]

The viewer must, says Collingwood, express emotions, just as the artist does, and he or she thereby becomes an artist in the very process of appreciating art. The artist shows the viewers of the work of art how to express the particular emotion that is expressed in the work. The value of art both for creators and consumers lies in its capacity to clarify and individuate specific emotions. When a sensitive viewer looks at, for example, a Van Gogh painting of a pair of old boots (see p. 36), the emotion he or she experiences will, ideally, match Van Gogh's:

> This experience of the spectator's does not repeat the comparatively poor experience of a person who merely looks at the subject; it repeats the richer and more highly organised experience of a person who has not only looked at it but has painted it as well.[29]

Collingwood's positive account of art proper can better be appreciated by setting it in contrast with two sorts of activity which he relegates to the category of 'art so-called': magic art and amusement art. For Collingwood, both art as magic and art as amusement should rightly be categorised as forms of craft, and not as art proper. Both fall within the technical theory of art. Both treat art as intimately related to emotion, but to its arousal rather than to its imaginative expression. Art as magic is Collingwood's name for works that are means to the preconceived end of arousing particular emotions, as in rituals. He does not mean the term 'magic' to be pejorative: magic is a means to the end of arousing emotions which are 'focused, and crystallised, consolidated into effective agents in practical life'.[30] These emotions are not discharged through the magic, whether it takes the form of a dance, a song or a painting, but rather channelled into the practical life of the society. He has in mind the 'magic' rituals of other societies, but also those objects and activities which have an analogous role in his own society. Thus, a patriotic song such as 'Rule Britannia' is a work of magical art in Collingwood's sense, since its purpose is to arouse particular sorts of patriotic feeling which may then be channelled into action. The heart stirred by the anthem emboldens the listener to perform noble deeds for the mother country. In such cases the desired effect of the music is not cathartic. Ideally the emotions are directed into socially appropriate action.

Magic art contrasts with amusement or entertainment art. Here again art evokes particular emotions. Yet in these cases the discharge of emotion is an end in itself:

> Magic is useful, in the sense that the emotions it excites have a practical function in the affairs of every day; amusement is not useful but only enjoyable because there is a watertight bulkhead between its world and the world of common affairs. The emotions generated by amusement run their course within this watertight compartment.[31]

Magic art serves a purpose, is 'utilitarian' in that sense. Amusement art is, in contrast, 'hedonistic'; it has no use apart from the generation of pleasurable feeling:

> It is as skilfully constructed as a work of engineering, as skilfully compounded as a bottle of medicine, to produce a determinate and preconceived effect, the evocation of a certain kind of emotion in a certain kind of audience; and to discharge this emotion within the limits of a make-believe situation.[32]

If taking a pill would produce the same preconceived effect as the work of amusement art, then the pill would serve the purpose equally well. Collingwood would no doubt have classified most of Alfred Hitchcock's films as entertainment art, not as art proper. Hitchcock was acutely aware of the likely effects of different cinematic devices on an audience's emotions, and manipulated these devices accordingly. This was often his primary aim. In the famous shower scene in *Psycho* (see p. 53), for example, in which a woman is stabbed to death by a maniac, every element of montage, soundtrack and camera angle is calculated to arouse

'Psycho' shower scene (1960), Alfred Hitchcock, courtesy of the Roland Grant Archive

horror – which it does. Hitchcock's own assessment of the film is revealing:

> My main satisfaction is that the film had an effect on the audiences, and I consider that very important. I don't care about the subject-matter; I don't care about the acting; but I do care about the pieces of film and the photography and the soundtrack and all the technical ingredients that made the audience scream. I feel it's tremendously satisfying for us to be able to use the cinematic art to achieve something of a mass emotion. And with *Psycho* we most definitely achieved this. It wasn't a message that stirred the audiences, nor was it a great performance or their enjoyment of the novel. They were aroused by pure film.[33]

It is clear from this that Hitchcock's intent, at least in this film, was the arousal of particular emotions in his audiences, not the clarification and expression of his own emotions. Such entertainment art has its place, Collingwood would say, but it is not art proper. It is interesting in this context to note that Hitchcock saw himself engaged in the same sort of enterprise as Shakespeare, in so far as both were designing works to achieve reactions from their audiences.[34] Shakespeare's plays, or at least some of them, are rather surprisingly included by Collingwood in his category of 'amusement art' on the grounds that they are works designed to please an Elizabethan audience.[35]

According to Collingwood, entertainment art carries with it serious dangers: its dominance in a society is a symptom of moral decay:

> Amusement becomes a danger to practical life when the debit it imposes on these stores of energy is too great to be paid off in the ordinary course of living. When this reaches a point of crisis, practical life or 'real' life, becomes emotionally bankrupt; a state of things which we describe by speaking of its intolerable dullness or calling it a drudgery. A moral disease has set in, whose symptoms are a constant craving for amusement and an inability to take any interest in the affairs of ordinary life, the necessary work of livelihood and social routine. A person in whom the disease has become chronic is a person with a more or less settled conviction that amusement is the only thing that makes life worth living. A society in which the disease is endemic is one in which most people feel some such conviction most of the time.[36]

Collingwood saw his own society as being dragged down by amusement art, much of it disseminated by cinema and the 'wireless'.

The definition of art, then, was for him not a logical puzzle to be solved like a crossword. By drawing the distinction between art proper and art so-called, he instead hoped to resist the descent into corrupt consciousness that he saw as characteristic of his age.

There are at least two major strands in *The Principles of Art*: the defence of both Expressionist and Idealist accounts of art. Collingwood is an Expressionist in so far as he defines art as the imaginative expression of emotion; at the same time he is an Idealist since at key points in the book he claims that a work of art need not exist as embodied in any particular material. It can exist purely in the mind of the artist. For example, he writes:

> A work of art need not be what we should call a real thing. It may be what we call an imaginary thing. A disturbance, or a nuisance, or a navy, or the like, is not created at all until it is created as a thing having its place in the real world. But a work of art may be completely created when it has been created as a thing whose only place is in the artist's mind.[37]

His point here seems to be that a work of art need not be tangible. It can exist merely as an idea in the head of the artist. Typically artists do make objects when they express their emotions artistically. Their involvement with the medium – whether it be paint, clay or some other material – can be integral to this. But these objects are always simply the means by which observers can construct the work for themselves in their own mind. The real work exists in the form of the ideas in the mind of its creator, and of the person appreciating the work.

For Collingwood, appreciating art involves imagination: 'A work of art proper is a total activity which the person enjoying it apprehends or is conscious of, by the use of his imagination.'[38] This imaginative activity is not, in the case of the visual arts, all visual – nor in Collingwood's view is it specifically visual at all. He takes Bernard Berenson's position that 'tactile values' should be central to our experience of painting. They are the imagined sensations brought about by experience of distance, space, mass, and so on within a painting:

> . . . what we get from looking at a picture is not merely the experience of seeing, or even partly seeing and partly imagining, certain visible objects; it is also, and in Mr. Berenson's opinion more importantly, the imaginary experience of certain complicated muscular movements.[39]

The viewer of Cézanne's painting *Lac d'Annecy* would, on Collingwood's account, have an imaginary experience of moving through the landscape, presumably even of crossing the depicted lake. This experience would ideally be close to the artist's experience while painting the work. What the viewer appropriately enjoys here is not the direct sensuous appreciation of the blues and greens, and the depicted forms, but rather an imaginative tactile experience. The viewer's experience is what is enjoyed, not simply the physical object, the painting in the gallery:

> . . . the value of any given work of art to a person properly qualified to appreciate its value is not the delightfulness of the sensuous elements in which as a work of art it actually consists, but the delightfulness of the imaginative experience which those sensuous elements awake in him. Works of art are only means to an end; the end is this total imaginative experience which they enable us to enjoy.[40]

The influence of the Italian philosopher Benedetto Croce (1866–1952) is evident throughout *The Principles of Art*. Both Croce and Collingwood thought of art in terms of expression, and particularly in terms of making imprecise feelings precise. They believed that the externalisation of a work wasn't essential to its being a work of art. They also believed that art was a language, construing 'language' in the broadest terms to include any self-conscious bodily activity by which emotion is expressed. Writing and speech are not the only form of language; painting, dancing or playing the violin can all be linguistic in this use of the term.

Whether or not Collingwood was entirely original in his formulation of his theory, the status of the theory should be judged by its ability to withstand critical attention, not by its source. The fact that many artists understand their own activity as the expression of emotion does not prove that Collingwood's account is true. Collingwood's practical knowledge of what painting involves lends a seriousness and at times profundity to comments he makes in the process of expounding his theory. Artists can, however, be mistaken about the nature of the activity in which they are engaged. A philosophical theory must be judged by its explanatory power and insight, but also by its ability to withstand counter-argument and attempted refutation. Here, Collingwood's theory, like Bell's, is vulnerable.

Collingwood's notion of art proper admits many things that are not obviously art; at the same time it excludes some paradigm cases of art. It includes too much because it seems to imply that any imaginative expression of emotion will automatically qualify as a work of art – a highly counter-intuitive position. Clearly the expression of an emotion need not be a work of art. Expression of emotion, even in the sense in which Collingwood uses the term

'expression', is surely not a sufficient condition for something's being a work of art. For example, transference and counter-transference between a psychotherapist and his or her client could well take the form of a vague, scarcely conscious feeling being refined into a precisely expressed emotion, yet few people would argue that it is therefore a work of art. Perhaps, though, in Collingwood's terminology, this would not constitute an imaginative expression of emotion. However, a similar point could be made from within Collingwood's theory: his description of the appropriate role of the viewer of a painting seems to turn that viewer into an artist. The viewer imaginatively re-expresses the emotion that lies within the work. If this is an accurate reading of Collingwood on this point – and his theory is notoriously slippery – then it is simply implausible. As T. M. Knox commented of Collingwood in a biographical sketch: '. . . in philosophy he had visions the validity of which he did not succeed in justifying to others by argument.'[41]

The theory, at the same time as admitting too much into the realm of art proper, excludes many paradigmatic works of art. Rigorous application of the comments about magic art, for example, would seem to prevent most of the greatest paintings of the Renaissance being works of art. Religious art's function is 'to evoke, and constantly re-evoke, certain emotions whose discharge is to be effected in the activities of everyday life'.[42] Altarpieces and other devotional paintings are created as the focus of prayer and with a particular function in mind. Are we then to say that, for example, *The Wilton Diptych* (*c*.1395–9) (see pp. 58–9) in

The Wilton Diptych, Richard II presented to the Virgin and Child by his Patron Saint John the Baptist and Saints Edward and Edmund (c.1395–9), courtesy of the National Gallery, London

the National Gallery in London is not really a work of art since its purpose was not to express an emotion but rather to evoke particular religious feelings and to be a prop in a ritual of private devotion? Its religious function was probably enhanced by the clever use of punched gold leaf, which accentuated key details when viewed by candlelight.[43] The baby Christ's halo, for instance, contains within it a crown of thorns and four nails, presumably included to evoke emotions about Christ's later suffering and crucifixion rather than forming part of the artist's clarification of an initially vague feeling.

A further criticism of Collingwood's account is that for him the question of whether or not a particular object or activity is a work of art turns entirely upon its aetiology: the history of how it came to be as it is. This history, however, may in some cases be unavailable to any living viewer. The sculpture of the little dancing man described by Collingwood could equally have been a work of craft. Looking at it won't tell us whether or not it was made to a preconceived plan. For Collingwood the question of whether or not something is a work of art cannot be answered by looking at it. Instead it must be answered by consideration of the state of mind of the artist. This point doesn't completely undermine the theory. It simply focuses on a practical difficulty about its application to disputes on whether or not a particular work merits the label art proper. Even if Collingwood is correct about what art is, his account will not provide us with a way of discriminating between art proper and art so-called. Take the case of Hitchcock's film *Psycho* discussed above. The fact that it involved superb crafts-manship in the design and execution of its major scenes in no way rules out the possibility of its being a work of art. As we have seen, art proper and craft – for Collingwood – are not mutually exclusive categories. The fact that Hitchcock chose to describe the film's success as lying in the manipulation of the emotions of his audiences does not prove conclusively that this is a correct description of the director's state of mind. Perhaps the film was indeed created by a process of refining and expressing an inchoate emotion. The problem is that, apart from considering the inconclusive evidence provided by a sensitive viewing of the film, we do not have any straightforward means of access to the relevant evidence.

Collingwood's theory, like Bell's, is insightful in many respects, but implausible as an answer to the general question 'What is art?' It is the conspicuous failure of such general theorising about art that led some philosophers to declare that the whole project of striving to define the term was misguided. Art, they claimed, is indefinable, and it is a logical mistake to seek the essence of it.

Chapter Three | Family Resemblances

Philosophers of art have traditionally set out on a quest to discover the grail of the essence of art. Some have even believed that if you can't find a defining feature, then you can't talk meaningfully about 'art' at all. 'Art', they thought, was the same as any term we use: if you can't define it, you don't really know what it means. And there is the deeper suspicion that perhaps 'art' doesn't mean anything at all. Perhaps all speculation about the nature of art is so much hot air.

Being able to recognise that some objects are art – Bellini's *Madonna of the Meadows*, Rodin's *The Kiss*, Alberto Giacometti's *Man Pointing*, and Jasper Johns' target paintings, for example – is not enough. You might unwittingly be using a clear concept. But knowing what 'art' means involves more than making appropriate judgements. It's not just a matter of applying a concept more or less correctly; it includes being able to spell it out in general terms. A general definition pinpoints the essence of art, the common feature that makes works of art *art* rather than something else.

The assumption that culturally created concepts such as 'justice' and 'virtue' (and, by extension, 'art') are amenable to this sort of definition goes back in the history of philosophy at least as far as Socrates, or rather Socrates as he appears in Plato's dialogues. There he repeatedly revealed other people's shortcomings as they tried to define key terms such as 'courage' or 'piety'. Giving a range of examples of the quality in question was never enough for Socrates. What he pursued relentlessly was a watertight definition that was immune to criticism. The implication was that others' inability to give a definition was a weakness in them rather than a logical feature of the subject in question.

In the wake of Ludwig Wittgenstein's thoughts about the nature of language, in the 1950s a number of philosophers began to ask whether this assumption was warranted, particularly when it came to defining 'art'. Perhaps the inadequacies of the various definitions so far proposed stemmed not so much from art's elusive qualities as from a logical mistake. Perhaps there was no such thing as the 'correct' definition of art, and the best that philosophers of art could then hope for was to reveal the complex patterns of overlapping resemblances between the things we called art. This view, that art cannot be defined by isolating its essential qualities, is the subject of this chapter.

In order to appreciate this position, consider a related example of an attempt to understand what makes an activity one thing rather than another. The example is that of the concept of 'game' and the question of how we decide whether or not an activity merits the description 'game'. In a memoir of time spent with Wittgenstein, his friend Norman Malcolm recounts the following incident:

Once after supper, Wittgenstein, my wife and I went for a walk on Midsummer Common. We talked about the movements of the bodies of the solar system. It occurred to Wittgenstein that the three of us should represent the movements of the bodies of the sun, earth, and moon, relative to one another. My wife was the sun and maintained a steady pace across the meadow; I was the earth and circled her at a trot. Wittgenstein took the most strenuous part of all, the moon, and ran around me while I circled my wife. Wittgenstein entered into this game with great enthusiasm and seriousness, shouting instructions at us as he ran. He became quite breathless and dizzy with exhaustion.[1]

This provides an example of an activity that might be considered a game.[2] Malcolm calls it 'this game'. But is it really a game? How do we decide the issue? We might begin by pointing out that it was engaged in for fun. This seems to be a common feature shared by many games. Not all games, however, are engaged in for fun. The manager Bill Shankly once said of football, 'It's not a matter of life and death. It's more serious than that.' So, although being engaged in for fun is a typical feature of games, it isn't a necessary feature of all games. Some games might not be fun at all, but would still be games. We still, for example, talk of gladiatorial combat as Roman games, but presumably these weren't fun for all those taking part.

Another approach might be to point out that what Wittgenstein and his friends were doing appeared to have rules. Perhaps all games have rules. In this case the rules seem to be that the players take on the roles of the sun, the earth and the moon. These rules determine their trajectories. But the rules are not written. And it is possible that within the same activity new dimensions could be added which could not have been foreseen at the start. For instance, the whole activity could have turned into something like a race. Or even a dance. But, if this is so, where are the rules? Can you have a game in which the rules are made up as you go along? Besides which, many activities which are governed by rules aren't games – sitting examinations and driving on the motorway, for example. So having rules could only be a necessary condition of an activity being a game, and so cannot be the essence of 'game'.

A different approach would be to compare the activity to paradigms of games. Here the most relevant examples might be games of make-believe. Certainly what the Cambridge trio were doing was in some sense playing a game of make-believe. So does this conclusively answer the question? Perhaps. But what, then, if somebody were to argue that what I have described was not a game at all? On what grounds could I confidently dispute the issue?

A widely held assumption about language is that if we fully understand the word 'game', then we should be able to specify what all games have in common. All games must have some essential element in common or else we would not be justified in calling them games at all. As we saw in Chapter One, Bell held such a view about the definition of 'visual art' when he wrote: 'For either all works of visual art have some common quality, or when we speak of "works of art" we gibber'.[3]

In his book *Philosophical Investigations*, and in his teaching, Wittgenstein suggested that, at least for some terms, the assumption of this sort of common denominator was misplaced. He called these 'family resemblance terms'. This metaphor of family resemblance reveals how we can make sense of a word like 'game' even though in practice we will not be able to find a single defining common denominator that all games share. Think of a family

– such as the Osmonds (see p. 64) – whose members are related by blood. One brother may share his father's temperament, and his eye and hair colour. Another brother may be more like his mother in terms of hair colour but not eye colour. A third might have his mother's smile, and his grandfather's eyes. There is probably no single distinctive feature that runs through the whole family of genetically related individuals, but nevertheless when we meet members of this family we can instantly recognise them as being related to one another. What allows us to do this is a pattern of overlapping and criss-crossing resemblances. This is the basis of Wittgenstein's notion of a family resemblance. It is perhaps best-revealed in his discussion of games. Like the members of the family, games have no single defining feature that is present in every case, no common essence. Rather what we find when we look at games of various kinds is a pattern of overlapping resemblances; similarities in some respects and not others. Here is the key passage from Wittgenstein's *Philosophical Investigations*:

> Consider for example the proceedings that we call 'games'. I mean board-games, card-games, ball-games, Olympic games, and so on. What is common to them all? – Don't say: "there *must* be something common, or they would not be called 'games'" – but *look and see* whether there is anything common to all – for if you look at them you will not see something that is common to *all*, but similarities, relationships, and a whole series of them at that. To repeat: don't think, but look! – look for example at board-games with their multifarious relationships. Now pass to card-games; here you may find many correspondences with the first group, but many common features drop out, and others appear. When we pass next to ball-games, much that is common is retained, but much is lost. – Are they all 'amusing'?

Compare chess with noughts and crosses. Or is there always winning and losing, or competition between players? Think of patience. In ball-games there is winning and losing; but when a child throws his ball at the wall and catches it again, this feature has disappeared. Look at the parts played by skill and luck; and at the difference between skill in chess and skill in tennis. Think now of games like ring-a-ring-a roses; here is the element of amusement, but how many other characteristic features had disappeared! And we can go through the many, many other groups of games in the same way; can see how similarities crop up and disappear.

And the result of this examination is: we see a complicated network of similarities overlapping and criss-crossing: sometimes overall similarities, sometimes similarities of detail.[4]

The implication of this passage is that 'game' cannot be defined, at least not in terms of necessary and sufficient conditions. The reason is, to use another of Wittgenstein's metaphors, that no single fibre runs the length of a piece of rope. This is part of Wittgenstein's wider attack on the view that for every concept there must be some essential feature common to all the things that fall under that concept. Such a view, he believed, was based on a misplaced 'craving for generality',[5] a craving which leads to a contemptuous attitude towards explanations which use a range of examples rather than generalisations. For Wittgenstein, family resemblance concepts, such as 'game' (or, for that matter, 'language'), could be adequately explained by presenting examples. They could never in principle be captured by any general definition couched in terms of necessary and sufficient conditions.

So, to return to the activity of Wittgenstein, Norman Malcolm and Mrs Malcolm on the banks of the Cam, if we want to determine whether or not what they were doing really was playing a game, then we won't be able to do this by consulting the common feature shared by all games. No such common feature exists. 'Game' has no essence. Actually, to talk of a common feature here is slightly misleading. It is obvious that, for example – as I implied several sentences ago – all games are activities; anything that is a game must, in some sense, be an activity. So the claim that games don't share a common feature is simply false. But being an activity is not the kind of common denominator that those who attempt to define 'game' are seeking. They want to find a common feature that allows us to identify all and only games, an essence of 'game' and not merely an unimportant necessary condition of something's being a game. To determine whether or not Wittgenstein and the Malcolms were playing a game, we might, using Wittgenstein's approach, examine the pattern of overlapping resemblances between what they were doing and what occurs in uncontroversial examples of games. On the basis of this pattern of overlapping resemblances, we might then argue that their activity was a game.

Wittgenstein urges those who are resistant to the idea that there is no essence of everything that goes under the name of 'game' to 'look and see'. It may be tempting to think that there *must* be a common feature shared by all games, but the truth is that we can use the word 'game' despite not being able to find a common denominator. To think otherwise is to be in the grip of a false theory of language.

This might all seem tangential to the question 'what is art?', a question to which Wittgenstein did not provide an answer. However, philosophers influenced by Wittgenstein (often labelled neo-Wittgensteinians) who have applied his thinking to the question have suggested that 'art' cannot be defined. 'Art' like 'game' is a family resemblance term. Consequently there is no single common essence shared by all works of art, so no simple definition is possible. Bell's assumption was, on this view, mistaken: we can talk meaningfully about 'art' or 'visual art', despite not being able to identify a single feature that all works of art share. Indeed, we have no alternative.

One of the earliest and most influential philosophers to take this line was Morris Weitz in his article 'The role of theory in aesthetics', first published in 1956.[6] Weitz declared that traditional aesthetic theory of the kind Bell attempted 'radically misconstrues the logic of the concept of art'.[7] It does this because it 'tries to define what cannot be defined'. He made the point in terms of what he called 'open' and 'closed' concepts. 'Art' is an open concept ('open concept' corresponds to Wittgenstein's notion of a family resemblance term). With an open concept there are some situations that require us to make a decision as to whether or not to extend the use of the concept to cover a new case. With a closed concept, necessary and sufficient conditions for the application of the concept can be given. For instance, to score a goal in soccer it is a necessary condition that you get the ball over the goal line, and a sufficient condition that the referee declares a goal to have been scored. Or, to give another example of a closed concept, within the context of a particular psychology experiment I might arbitrarily close the concept 'intelligent' by stipulating that by this term I mean 'having scored more than 100 on an I.Q. test'. Once that stipulation has been made, factual analysis of test results will reveal whether or not an individual is intelligent for the purpose of the experiment. An open concept like 'art', in contrast, allows for the possibility of new and unforeseen cases which do not necessarily share a presumed common feature. With an open concept, language-users must decide – perhaps not explicitly, but at least through their practice – rather than discern whether or not to admit the new case as falling within the concept.

One of Weitz's main arguments against definition is that attempting to define art in the traditional manner (that is, closing the concept) 'forecloses on the very conditions of creativity in the arts'.[8] He declares that 'the very expansive, adventurous character of art, its ever-present changes and novel creations, makes it logically impossible to ensure any set of defining properties'.[9] Notice, here, that he is not saying that 'art' is difficult to define. He is claiming that it is *logically impossible* to define. Part of the problem of attempting to define art is that artists often react against dominant conceptions of art, deliberately presenting works which go beyond what is traditionally conceived as art. As Tony Godfrey has pointed out:

> Art is a concept: it does not exist as a precisely definable physical type of thing, as elephants or chairs do. Since it became self-conscious, aware that it was a special category, art has often played with this 'conceptual' status.[10]

That, for example, is in part what Marcel Duchamp was doing with his readymades. In more recent times, the Tate Gallery in London included Tracey Emin's *My Bed* (see p. 75) in its exhibition of works of art shortlisted for the Turner Prize (1999). *My Bed* is a real bed, the actual bed, we are told, in which Emin contemplated suicide, together with her dirty bedclothes and bedroom clutter (including soiled knickers, empty vodka bottles, condom packets and tampons). Closing the concept of art might prevent such works from becoming works of art since they would not, by their very nature, conform with the pre-existing notion of what art is (or at least would not conform with pre-twentieth-century concepts of art). Duchamp's *Fountain* and Emin's *My Bed* are real objects, not specifically works of art, and so, on most traditional views, should not be counted as works of art. Not enough seems to have been done to them to justify treating them as artifacts imbued with complex meanings, for example. Furthermore, neither was presented with a view to their aesthetic qualities being appreciated. Some will perhaps say, 'And so much the better if such trivia were recognised as nothing to do with art.' And yet the possibility of creating new works that challenge preconceptions about what art is seems to have been an important pre-condition for development in all the arts. This is true whether or not we happen to approve of the new works which emerge as challenges to the tradition. Also, a fact that is rarely noticed is that if we are to affirm the artist's right to produce challenges to the tradition on grounds of artistic freedom, we should probably also affirm the right of artists to continue to repeat these challenges in scarcely altered form, as some argue that Tracey Emin and many of her contemporaries do.

Weitz believed that it would always be a mistake to try to specify what should count as art, and that the practical individual decisions about which objects were and which were not art should be made by the experts, usually by professional critics:

New conditions (cases) have constantly arisen and will undoubtedly constantly arise; new art forms, new movements will emerge, which will demand decisions on the part of those interested, usually

My Bed (1999), Tracey Emin, © Tracey Emin/courtesy of White Cube

professional critics, as to whether the concept should be extended or not. Aestheticians may lay down similarity conditions but never necessary and sufficient ones for the correct application of the concept. With 'art' its conditions of application can never be exhaustively enumerated since new cases can always be envisaged or created by artists, or even nature, which would call for a decision on someone's part to extend or to close the old or to invent a new concept.[11]

Weitz did not restrict his attack to the quest to define art. He made the same sort of points about sub-concepts of art such as 'painting' and 'portraiture'. We can choose to close any of these sub-concepts arbitrarily, but only at the risk of shutting down the very conditions of new creation. For instance, the 'painting' sub-concept of art could have arbitrarily been closed so that paintings were by definition representational. The consequence of such a stipulation would, on Weitz's account, have been that the Abstract Expressionists' decision to react against a tradition of representational painting would have put them outside the realm of painting. The work of Rothko, Pollock and Newman could not be accommodated within that closed sub-concept of representational painting. Creative oppositional reaction to existing tradition – so typical of the history of art – would then not be part of art, but would fall outside the concept. This is what Weitz means when he says that closing the concept of art, or any of its sub-concepts, would foreclose on artistic creativity.

That such creativity is highly valued in the Western tradition is certainly true. We tend to value what has not been done before. Indeed, it could be argued that a great artist must exhibit this sort of creativity to be great. This raises the questions, why do we, and indeed why should we, value such creativity? Weitz doesn't address these questions. However, Alfred Lessing, in the context of a discussion of the aesthetic status of forgeries, does. His answer is this:

> art has and must have a history. If it did not, if artists were concerned only with making beautiful pictures, poems, symphonies, etc., the possibilities for the creation of aesthetically pleasing works of art would soon be exhausted. We would (perhaps) have a number of lovely paintings, but we should soon grow tired of them, for they would all be more or less alike. But artists do not seek merely to produce works of beauty. They seek to produce *original* works of beauty. And when they succeed in achieving this originality we call their works great not only because they are beautiful but because they have also unlocked, both to artists and to appreciators, unknown and unexplored realms of beauty. Men like Leonardo, Rembrandt, Haydn, Goethe, and Vermeer are great not merely because of the excellence of their works but also because of their creative originality which goes on to inspire other artists and leads through them to new and aesthetically valuable developments in the history of art. It is, in fact, this search for creative originality which ensures the continuation and significance of such a history in the first place.[12]

Neither Weitz's nor Lessing's conclusions about the value of creativity and originality are as obviously true as they imply. The fact that great artists have found outlets for their creativity in extremely constrained forms, such as the haiku or the fugue, suggests that restricting artistic choices does not prevent creativity of a kind which can inspire and astound. It might, however, prevent art from lurching off in completely new directions. The loss of this possibility would indeed be great. In other words, closing the concept of 'art' might only foreclose on *some* kinds of creativity, those usually associated with avant-garde Western art. A naturalistic explanation of the value we attach to new and previously unthought of developments in art is that human beings on the whole relish novelty in whatever realm. This point was made forcefully by Edmund Burke in the opening section of his *A Philosophical Enquiry into the Origin of our Ideas of the Sublime and Beautiful* (1757):

> The first and the simplest emotion which we discover in the human mind, is Curiosity. By curiosity, I mean whatever desire we have for, or whatever pleasure we take in novelty. We see children perpetually running from place to place to hunt out something new; they catch with great eagerness, and with very little choice, at whatever comes before them; their attention is engaged by every thing, because everything has, in that stage of life, the charm of novelty to recommend it.[13]

Although Burke thought such curiosity the most superficial of all emotions, he acknowledged that:

> Some degree of novelty must be one of the materials in every instrument which works upon the mind; and curiosity blends itself more or less with all our passions.[14]

New developments in art have the potential to satisfy cravings for novelty; though if they are merely new and nothing more, then they are unlikely to occupy us for long.

Assuming that we do indeed value new developments in art, was Weitz correct in thinking that a traditional definition would necessarily foreclose on such creativity? He presents this point as if it were a conceptual truth. Yet were someone to come up with a broad enough definition of art, a definition nevertheless in terms of necessary and sufficient conditions, this could in principle leave open the possibility of new developments. In other words, Weitz does not prove, but rather takes for granted, that any traditional definition of art will foreclose on creativity. However, it is not the fact that such a definition involves closing the concept that presents problems, but rather that in general those who have produced traditional theories of what art is – such as Bell and Collingwood – have, as it happens, given quite narrow definitions, definitions which would indeed conspicuously limit creativity in art if taken as binding for all time rather than as revisable responses to the art of their time.[15] The force of Weitz's point derives, then, from the narrowness of actual definitions of art, and is not the logical point about the concept of art that he takes it to be.

Furthermore, even if we concede that 'art' is and should remain an open concept, it does not in any way follow that the sub-concepts of art must be kept open to avoid foreclosing on creativity. If, for example, collage did not comply with the closed conditions of entry stipulated for the 'painting' sub-concept of art, then we could quite simply stipulate a new closed sub-concept of art, namely 'collage'. In other words, Weitz's belief about the detrimental effects on creativity in the arts that would follow from closing the concept 'art' in no way implies similar detrimental effects resulting from closing its sub-concepts.

How, then, according to Weitz, would we determine whether or not a controversial object such as Mark Wallinger's *A Real Work of Art* – the racehorse discussed in the Introduction – was what it purports to be, namely a real work of art? Weitz gives an example from the sub-concept 'the novel' to show how his theory explains what happens in practice:

> Consider questions like "Is Dos Passos' *U.S.A.* a novel?," "Is V. Woolf's *To The Lighthouse* a novel?" "Is Joyce's *Finnegans Wake* a novel?" On the traditional view, these are construed as factual problems to be answered yes or no in accordance with the presence or absence of defining properties. But certainly this is not how any of these questions is answered. Once it arises, as it has many times in the development of the novel from Richardson to Joyce (e.g. "Is Gide's *The School for Wives* a novel or a diary?") what is at stake is no factual analysis concerning necessary and sufficient properties but a decision as to whether the work under examination is similar in certain respects to other works, already called "novels", and consequently warrants the extension of the concept to cover the new case.[16]

Applying the same sort of reasoning to the case of Wallinger's horse, Weitz would have to say that there are many resemblances between the racehorse and conventionally accepted works of art. Despite initial appearances that the horse is not an artifact, it might be pointed out that it only looks the way it does because of a great deal of selective breeding, training and grooming. It is certainly beautiful and worth looking at. However, on the other hand, it is a living animal and so in this respect differs from accepted paradigms of works of art. On the basis of the pattern and kind of criss-crossing and overlapping resemblances between the horse and paradigm instances of art, we as a community of language-users must take a decision as to whether it is a work of art or not – perhaps a work of living sculpture. Similarly, with Damien Hirst's *Mother and Child Divided* – which consists of a cow and its calf sawn in half and the two bits of each animal preserved in formaldehyde in glass tanks – the question of whether or not it is art would be decided, on Weitz's theory, by considering the pattern and type of resemblances holding between the sculpture and other, accepted works of art. In fact, it seems, in the cases of *A Real Work of Art* and of *Mother and Child Divided*, at least the sub-section of society we call the art world has decided that they *are* art, just as, in Weitz's example, Gide's book was deemed a novel, and so a work of art. In Weitz's words 'we' have chosen to accept Gide's book as a novel. But this raises important questions, which he doesn't answer, as to who 'we' are.

Furthermore, Weitz offers no scheme for deciding what is to count as a *relevant* resemblance. Resemblance is a slippery notion. Anything can be said to resemble anything else in some sense. The Empire State Building and a pin resemble each other in that they are both designed objects with specific functions. They are both made from inorganic materials; they are both tapered. And so on. Not only will we have to be able to say what counts as a *relevant* resemblance, but we will also have to know how to weight this resemblance against what appear to be relevant differences between the new putative artwork and the paradigm case. So there is not only the problem of whose decision is to count in this area, but also the problem of the criteria they use to determine the relevance and weight of perceived resemblances between the putative artwork and the paradigm cases. This presents serious problems for anyone attempting to apply Weitz's account of art.

A further problem for Weitz is how he can explain the existence of art at all. Even if we concede that new works of art gain their status because of their resemblances to paradigm works, we will still be left with the problem of how art ever became established as a category. With the very first art, there could have been no paradigm of art with which to compare it.

Even if we could specify the respects in which relevant resemblances between paradigm and putative works hold, and could get around the problem of how the very first art achieved the status of art, Weitz's conclusions would be far too strong on the basis of the evidence he provides. This is the most serious philosophical criticism of the argument he gives for his conclusion. He maintains that attempts to define art are 'logically misbegotten'.[17] However, all he offers in support of this conclusion are, first, the fact that all previous attempts to define art have been conspicuous failures, open to counter-example and counter-argument; and, second, that the Wittgensteinian notion of a family resemblance term adequately and plausibly explains these failures. But, even if we accept these points, it does not follow that art *necessarily* cannot be defined. It only follows that the hypothesis that it cannot be defined is a plausible one (which it is). Weitz, however, offers no conclusive proof of the indefinability of art and its sub-concepts. He does bring in the further argument about creativity and the concept of art. But, as we have seen, this rests on the dubious assumption that creativity would be ruled out were we to close the concept of art or any of its sub-concepts.

If Weitz is correct about the nature of art, it would seem to follow that all past art theory was a waste of effort, and scarcely worth reading now. He is, however, more generous than this. He argues that the great art theorists of the past, while searching for a definition of 'art', were in fact indirectly making a case for paying attention to particular elements in the art form concerned:

> To understand the role of aesthetic theory is not to conceive it as definition, logically doomed to failure, but to read it as summaries of

seriously made recommendations to attend in certain ways to certain features of art.[18]

Within each attempt at definition lies 'a debate over and argument for emphasising or centring upon some particular feature of art which has been neglected or perverted'.[19] On this account, the value of Bell's theory is that it draws attention to formal aspects of painting. As Weitz puts it, what lies behind the formula 'art is significant form' is this:

> In an age in which literary and representational elements have become paramount in painting, *return* to the plastic ones since these are indigenous to painting. Thus, the role of the theory is not to define anything but to use the definitional form, almost epigrammatically, to pinpoint a crucial recommendation to turn our attention once again to the plastic elements in painting.[20]

The value of Collingwood's theory was, by the same principle, that it encouraged those who were impressed by it to pay more attention to the process of clarifying and expressing emotion in art. This is certainly a way of reading traditional aesthetic theory. But it ignores what the authors of such theory were trying to do. As we have seen, Bell and Collingwood were explicit about their intentions; they were both attempting to define art.

The philosopher Maurice Mandelbaum responded to Weitz's anti-essentialist line on the definition of art by pointing out that if we are to take seriously Wittgenstein's pronouncements about family resemblances, then we should notice that what members of a family have in common is a biological genetic connection. It is this attribute that causes the pattern of overlapping physical resemblances clearly visible to the viewer. Wittgenstein could quite easily have used a different metaphor, as he did for instance with the metaphor of the overlapping strands in a piece of rope. Mandelbaum's point, however, is that Wittgenstein's insistence that we 'look and see' whether games have anything in common pushes our attention entirely on to *exhibited* attributes of the activities we call games. Mandelbaum's suggestion is that, just as there is a non-exhibited common feature of a family (the genetic connection), so, analogously, there might be a non-exhibited property shared by all games, or indeed all works of art. Such a possibility cannot be ruled out as a conceptual impossibility.

Mandelbaum was sceptical about the basis of Weitz's anti-essentialist conclusions, and believed it was worth searching for some non-exhibited relational feature that all artworks shared. It is important to realise that this does not amount to a refutation of Weitz's position, only a toning down of its conclusion. It leaves open the possibility that 'art' is indeed a family resemblance term. What it challenges is the view that we can know in advance of attempting a definition of 'art' that our project is necessarily doomed to failure. Weitz's arguments for his position are simply that past attempts at definition have been conspicuous failures and, more importantly, given the central value of creativity in art, closing the concept would foreclose on one of the practice's most important features. The most that can reasonably be concluded from these two points is that art might be a family resemblance term, and that this is the most plausible hypothesis in the circumstances. If, however, as with an actual family resemblance, there is a non-exhibited common property that makes all works of art art, then a theory of art in the traditional essentialist sense is a genuine possibility. George Dickie's Institutional Theory of art, which we'll be examining in the next chapter, is a theory that purports to explain art with reference to just such a non-exhibited common property.

Chapter Four | Institutional Contexts

Damien Hirst's *The Physical Impossibility of Death in the Mind of Someone Living* (1991) (see pp. 88–9) is a dead tiger shark in a large tank made of glass and steel. The shark is suspended in a five per cent solution of formaldehyde. There is little about this work, apart from its title, to distinguish it from a zoological specimen, one which could equally be displayed in a natural history museum. The main element of the work – the shark – hasn't noticeably been altered, but is just a large dead animal. The tank is unremarkable. Yet this has been hailed as an important work of art, one of the major works by one of the most successful British artists of recent times. Like much of Hirst's art it examines aspects of our relationship with death, both through its metaphorical implications, given by the title, and through the very fact that it presents us immediately with a real dead animal. The subject is a traditional one. The medium is not.

The Physical Impossibility of Death in the Mind of Someone Living (1989), Damien Hirst, © Damien Hirst/courtesy of Science Ltd

How can this be art? What has brought about this change of the shark's status? Even if the subject matter is familiar, there is still the mystery of how the artist could have turned such a thing – a naturally occurring animal – into a work of art. The animal itself is there, not a representation of it. The mystery is similar to that initiated by Marcel Duchamp with his *Fountain*; dead animals could also be thought of as readymades. Indeed, one of the ways in which

artists in the late twentieth century played variations on the Duchampian move is, as we have seen already with Alys's peacock and Wallinger's horse, to use animals – living and dead – rather than machine-made objects in their work. Maurizio Cattelan's *Novecento (Twentieth century)* (see p. 86), to take a further example, consists of a dead and partly stuffed horse suspended from the ceiling in a sling. Its legs have been extended to make it appear more pathetic. The title invites us to find analogies between the horse and the century.

Like the approach discussed in the previous chapter, the Institutional Theory of art has an answer to this mystery, the mystery of how it is that machine-made objects, animals, and even people can be transformed into works of art. That is one of its greatest strengths. Indeed, the Institutional Theory was devised in conscious response to post-Duchampian developments in twentieth-century art such as Dadaism, pop art, found art and happenings. It treats works like *The Physical Impossibility of Death in the Mind of Someone Living* as central, even paradigm, cases of works of art. Its main defender, the American philosopher George Dickie, first formulated the theory in the late 1960s and early 1970s, although he has modified it several times since then.

What the Institutional Theory stresses is not the look of a work of art, but rather its context: how it has been treated by whoever created it, and by those who exhibit and appreciate it. It is a theory that explains what works of art have in common by drawing our attention to their non-exhibited, relational qualities. Some people in our society have the capacity to confer the status of 'artwork' on any artifact. That is the essence of the theory. The history of how an object has been treated rather than anything visibly detectable is the central factor in determining whether or not it is a work of art. One way of characterising this type of theory is to describe it as a *procedural* theory of art. This is a terminology popularised by the philosopher Stephen Davies.[1] He contrasts procedural definitions with *functional* definitions. Procedural definitions account for something's being a work of art by referring to social practices which change its status, rather than any intrinsic features of the work in question. Functional definitions of art concentrate on the purposes that works of art serve, such as to express emotion or to stimulate aesthetic pleasure. Bell and Collingwood's theories of art are functionalist in this sense; Dickie's Institutional Theory of art is procedural.[2]

The suggestion that what makes something a work of art may not be visible to the eye was made in an important article, 'The artworld', by the philosopher and art critic Arthur Danto, an article which influenced Dickie. Stirred in particular by Andy Warhol's *Brillo Boxes* (essentially copies of cardboard Brillo boxes made from painted plywood) (see p. 92), Danto raised the question of what it is about such objects that makes them works of art when they appear no different from real things:

> To mistake an artwork for a real object is no great feat when an artwork is the real object one mistakes it for. The problem is how to avoid such errors, or to remove them once they are made.[3]

He suggests that it is *theory* that makes something a work of art, not some visible element of it: 'To see something as art requires something that the eye cannot descry – an atmosphere of artistic theory, a knowledge of the history of art: an artworld.'[4]

This is the difference between Warhol's *Brillo Box* and its near cousins, the Brillo boxes stacked in a warehouse or supermarket. It is the artistic theory with which Warhol's boxes are connected that gives them their art status, not anything visually distinguishing them from their more mundane counterparts, such as the fact that Warhol's boxes were made of plywood rather than of cardboard:

> What in the end makes the difference between a Brillo box and a work of art consisting of a Brillo box is a certain theory of art. It is the theory

24 GIANT SIZE PKGS.
New!
Brillo
soap pads
WITH RUST RESISTER
SHINES ALUMINUM FAST
24 GIANT SIZE PKGS.
New!
Brillo
soap pads
WITH RUST RESISTER

that takes it up into the world of art, and keeps it from collapsing into the real object which it is (in a sense of *is* other than artistic identification). Of course, without the theory, one is unlikely to see it as art, and in order to see it as part of the artworld, one must have mastered a good deal of artistic theory as well as a considerable amount of the history of recent New York painting. It could not have been art fifty years ago.[5]

This is a recurrent theme in Danto's work; the idea that visually indistinguishable objects may have very different properties, and that those properties may be determined by the context of their presentation. For example, he opens his book *The Transfiguration of the Commonplace* with a thought experiment that would not be out of place in a story by Jorge Luis Borges. We are to imagine an exhibition of visually indiscernible paintings, each consisting of a square of red paint. Though visually indiscernible, different paintings have different subject matter. So one is 'The Israelites Crossing the Red Sea', another is 'Red Square', another, painted by an embittered disciple of Matisse, is 'Red Table Cloth', and so on. As Danto points out, the catalogue for this exhibition would be monotonous (in more than one sense), 'since everything looks the same as everything else, even though the reproductions are of paintings that belong to such diverse genres as historical painting, psychological portraiture, landscape, geometrical abstraction, religious art, and still life'.[6]

Danto's imaginary pictures are different paintings, despite their visual indiscernibility. And he is surely right that visually indistinguishable objects can, nevertheless, have different artistic properties. Think of how we might react if we were to discover that, for example, Jackson Pollock's painting *Summertime* was in fact a parody of his work, produced by a lesser artist for a bet. The marks on the canvas remain the same, but the artistic qualities that the work has do not. In the context of Pollock's *oeuvre*, this canvas had certain expressive qualities, whereas in the context of the parodist's work the principal qualities are of imitation and exaggeration. What the painting is about has changed. If the painting were by Pollock, then presumably it would be about the process of applying paint, and perhaps metaphorically about summertime. If by the parodist, it would be about Pollock's painting style. Furthermore, if you accept that there is no such thing as the innocent eye, it becomes plausible to say not just that the context of presentation has changed, but that what the viewer sees in each case is actually different. Seeing, as philosophers of science are quick to point out, is a theory-laden activity. What this means is that there is much more to vision than the image that falls on the back of your retinas. What you know and believe affects what you see. Your expectations and knowledge don't just help you to understand and interpret what you see, they in part help you to construct and categorise what you see. In his book *Ways of Seeing*, John Berger makes this point neatly by presenting a reproduction of a painting by Van Gogh. The painting shows birds flying over a cornfield. On the following page it appears with the caption 'This is the last painting that Van Gogh painted before he killed himself.'[7] The knowledge that Van Gogh committed suicide shortly after the painting was completed changes how the picture looks. The crows flying over the cornfield, for example, appear far more threatening than they would otherwise have felt. As Berger puts it:

'It is hard to define exactly how the words have changed the image but undoubtedly they have.'[8] The point is that pictures producing identical retinal images or, as in this case, one picture seen at different times by a viewer with different knowledge about the picture can look different.

Dickie developed his Institutional Theory of art from Danto's insights (although Danto has distanced himself from Dickie's theory). Maurice Mandelbaum's suggestion, discussed in Chapter Three – that art might be definable at a non-exhibited level – also influenced him. His Institutional Theory in its earlier and most influential form is this:

> A work of art in the classificatory sense is (1) an artifact (2) a set of the aspects of which has had conferred upon it the status of candidate for appreciation by some person or persons acting on behalf of a certain social institution (the artworld).[9]

This quasi-legalistic definition needs to be unpacked. First, and perhaps most controversially, Dickie's definition of art is only concerned with a 'classificatory' sense of 'art'. It is entirely neutral on questions of whether something's being a work of art implies that it has any value. 'Classificatory' stands in oppostion to the 'evaluative' theories, such as Bell's and Collingwood's, which make it very clear that if something falls within the category of art it has some value to us, it is not trivial, it is worthy of our attention and contemplation. For Bell and Collingwood, the value of art is moral as well as aesthetic. For Dickie, the question of what art is can be separated out from the question of which sorts of thing we should hold in high esteem or aim to engage with. For him, to recognise that something is a work of art does not imply that it has any value whatsoever. It may be utterly trivial and worthless, but still art rather than non-art. As he puts it, when discussing the question of the limits of what can be an artifact: 'One *can* make a work of art out of a sow's ear, but that does not necessarily make it a silk purse.'[10] Dickie's approach is like that of a Martian anthropologist trying to categorise the different sorts of practice he finds on Earth. He arrives, looks around at what human beings happen to describe as art and then builds a theory that explains what all these things have in common. All that they end up having in common is a certain sort of relationship to the artworld. The apparent circularity of this approach is something we'll return to.

Unlike almost all of his predecessors Dickie is only interested in a neutral classificatory sense of the art question. This is sometimes overlooked by his cruder critics who accuse him of claiming that members of the artworld have the Midas touch, turning everything they come into contact with into gold. This is a misleading image because Dickie is clear that, even if members of the artworld have this almost magical ability to transform everyday objects into works of art, this in no way implies anything about the relative value – aesthetic, artistic or otherwise – of the products of their transformations.

The first requirement of Dickie's definition is that a work of art be an artifact. He makes artifactuality a necessary condition. Obviously it can't be a sufficient condition since that would mean that every artifact was automatically a work of art. The artifactuality condition and the conferral-of-status condition are jointly sufficient for something's being a work of art. If both conditions are met, then the artifact with conferred status is guaranteed to be a work of art, or 'artwork' as he terms it. He uses the word 'artifact' here in a special sense. It usually means any object which has in some sense been worked on or modified by human intervention. There is no problem for traditional artworks meeting this requirement. For instance, paintings and sculptures are clearly artifacts in the usual sense of the term. Almost every theory of art ever proposed makes artifactuality in this sense a necessary condition for something's being a work of art. It is by this stipulation that naturally occurring objects such as sunsets and interestingly shaped carrots are ruled out as non-art (unless, of course, you believe them to be the work of a Divine Artist). For Dickie, however, at least in his early formulation of his theory, artifactuality is something that can be conferred upon natural objects, even carrots and sunsets, without otherwise modifying them.

Although in most cases artifactuality will be achieved in the usual way, by altering raw materials, this is not the only way in which it can be achieved. A piece of driftwood washed up on the beach unaltered by human hand could become an artifact in Dickie's sense simply by being, for example, displayed in a gallery. The driftwood needn't be visually interesting, nor does it need to be changed physically by human intervention. Even pointing to it on the beach, and inviting others to view it in a particular way, might be enough to make it an artifact in his sense. This makes clear that Dickie's notion of an artifact is potentially broad enough not to rule out any object (or idea) that is presented as a potential work of art. So his first necessary condition in his definition does not appear to limit what can become art in any significant way. This might seem like a weakness in Dickie's theory. But advocates of the theory stress that – although Dickie's is a traditional definition of art in that it provides necessary and sufficient conditions for something's being a work of art – the definition of art does not suffer from the problem that Weitz diagnosed: it does not 'foreclose on creativity'.

The second condition in his definition, which Dickie presents as a further necessary condition for something's being a work of art, is more complex than the first. It turns on the notion of the conferral of the status of being a 'candidate for appreciation'. The word 'status' is potentially confusing here, because – in line with his interest only in a classificatory sense of 'art' – Dickie means it in a neutral sense. When people talk of 'status symbols' the word 'status' implies 'high status'. This is not the sense in which Dickie is using the word here. It is more like the neutral use of the term when you are asked to give your marital status.

According to Dickie's earlier theory, the status is conferred on an artifact by the equivalent of a christening or dubbing ceremony. Some member or members of the art world present it as a 'candidate for appreciation'. As with a christening, this only makes sense within a framework of historically evolved conventions and mutual understandings. The process needn't be a formal one as the analogy of a christening might suggest. It can be as simple as an artist treating an object in a certain way, or a gallery including the object in an exhibition. The key point is that what makes something a work of art on this account is its relation to a particular, rather loosely connected set of practices: it is a relational property.

According to Dickie, the member or members of the art world don't confer the status on the whole artifact, but only on some aspects of it. This point about aspects is simply to avoid the criticism that, for example, the string on the back of a painting is not usually an essential aspect of it as a work of art. It can be removed or replaced without affecting the work of art. Nor is the frame of a painting typically an integral part of the artwork, though there are exceptions, such as Howard Hodgkin's frames which are sometimes painted over by the artist. In every case it is only some aspects of the object or event that are presented as the essential artwork.

'Candidate for appreciation' is a rather vague phrase. The word 'candidate' is included because Dickie does not want to insist that an object or event actually has to be appreciated by anyone in order for it to be a work of art. So it only has to be presented as a possible object for appreciation, and may fail to be appreciated. This is consistent with his separation of questions of aesthetic or artistic value from questions of whether or not something is a work of art. Quality is not the issue. For Dickie, the art question is the question of the category something belongs to, not whether it was worth making or displaying.

The process of conferral is not as mysterious as it might sound. In practice, conferral is often achieved by displaying the artifact in a gallery, or performing the work in a theatre or concert hall. The person or people who carry out the conferral are members of the art world. But it is important to realise that Dickie is using his term 'artworld' in a much broader sense than it is usually used. The art world for Dickie is not a group of art dealers, gallery organisers and auction houses. It includes anyone who thinks he or she is a member of it. Anyone who thinks of him- or herself as an artist is by that fact a member of the art world. In most cases the person who confers the status will be the artwork's creator at the time of creation, although this need not be the case, as with readymades and found art. This point is worth emphasising as many of Dickie's detractors fix on the word 'artworld' and assume that he is putting forward an elitist theory that gives special powers to a clique of art *cognoscenti*. In *The Painted Word*, Tom Wolfe half-seriously itemised the art world members who he thought between them defined taste in modern art:

... about 750 culturati in Rome, 500 in Milan, 1,750 in Paris, 1,250 in London, 2,000 in Berlin, Munich and Dusselfdorf, 3,000 in New York, and perhaps 1,000 scattered about the rest of the known world. That is the art world, approximately 10,000 souls – a mere hamlet! – restricted to *les beaux mondes* of eight cities.[11]

According to Wolfe, these 10,000 art world members more or less determine what is to count as significant art. Dickie's notion of the art world is nothing like this. Nor is his notion of a work of art restrictive or exclusive. In fact he leaves the concept of art so open that it allows the possibility of anyone at all making a work of art, regardless of their level of skill, knowledge of art practices, awareness of the art scene, or visual acumen. Although his is a definition in the traditional sense, it is a definition that excludes virtually no putative work of art from achieving the full status of artwork. The people who confer the status of artwork are not a specially trained elite. The category is much broader than that.

When someone has a university degree conferred upon them at a graduation ceremony, their status changes as the result of actions of those empowered to confer degrees. This change of status does not make the graduate visibly different, but nevertheless he is different. The same is true of artifacts that are transformed into artworks.

Returning to the example of Damien Hirst's shark, the Institutional Theory illuminates how what appears to be simply a biological specimen can have become a work of art. The shark in its tank fulfils the artifactuality condition in the ordinary sense. The tank has been constructed, the shark positioned in formalde-hyde, and so on. If you are in doubt as to whether a shark can be considered an artifact, in Dickie's sense of the term, it is in the same position as a piece of driftwood discussed earlier. Even if Hirst hadn't placed the shark within the tank and given it a title, the shark could have been considered an artifact. The artist could simply have conferred the status of artifact upon the shark by placing the shark in a gallery, as Mark Wallinger conferred the status of artwork on the horse *A Real Work of Art*. Damien Hirst is a member of the artworld in Dickie's sense; he is an active artist. He has conferred the status of 'candidate for appreciation' on some aspects of the shark and its case. Presumably the formaldehyde is not a constitutive element of the artwork, and could be replaced if, as is rumoured to be happening, the shark begins to decay (although this raises the question of whether the gradual decay of the shark over time was an aspect of the artwork, particularly as some of Hirst's work has involved decaying animal flesh, most notably in *A Thousand Years* which included a rotting cow's head on which maggots fed, matured into flies, bred, and then were zapped by an electric fly killer).

Notice that, even if you despise Hirst's work and deem it unworthy of the title 'art', you are using 'art' in an evaluative sense. Dickie is only concerned with the neutral 'classificatory' sense of 'art'. In that sense, the work is a work of art since, whether or not it is actually appreciated (and it surely has been), the work has been presented for appreciation. The theory explains why it is a work of art, even if you think it a bad work. It is for art critics to determine which works are good or bad. But the philosophical point is that it is the history of what has been done to the object rather than any particular visual feature of it that has transformed it into a work of art.

While Dickie's theory can cope well with recent challenging 'anxious objects' such as Hirst's, with their self-conscious links to artistic traditions, it is less convincing when applied to cases of outsider art, a heterogeneous category of art produced well outside anything that could be labelled the art world. The psychiatrist Hans Prinzhorn (1886–1933) collected an astonishing range of work produced by the mentally ill which culminated in his influential book *The Artistry of the Insane*. Most of the contributors to this book would have had no conception of themselves as members of the art world. The artist Jean Dubuffet, inspired by Prinzhorn's book, amassed a collection of intriguing drawings, paintings and other artifacts produced by outsiders of various kinds. He coined the term *art brut* to cover work

> characterised by spontaneity and pronounced inventiveness, owing as little as possible to conventional art and cultural clichés, and created by anonymous people outside professional artistic circles.[12]

Champions of such works have argued that far from being peripheral to art, or merely an influence on it, this sort of creation is a truer art, more directly in touch with the sources of artistic creativity than the self-consciously produced art of the mainstream. Dubuffet emphasised the purity of the artistic impulse in outsider art:

> We are witness here to a completely pure artistic operation, raw, brut, and entirely reinvented in all of its phases solely by means of the artists' own impulses. It is thus an art which manifests an unparalleled inventiveness, unlike cultural art, with its chameleon- and monkey-like aspects.[13]

To bring out the implications for Dickie's theory of such outsider art, I want to look more closely at two outsider artists whose work has been absorbed into the mainstream history of art: the painter Alfred Wallis and the photographer E. J. Bellocq.

Alfred Wallis's naïve paintings of Cornish seacapes and ships (see, for example, p. 107) have been recognised as significant contributions to the art of the twentieth century. They have been collected by the Tate Gallery and the Museum of Modern Art in New York, amongst others, and are usually given a prominent place in histories of English modernist painting. Wallis was an elderly retired merchant seaman with psychiatric problems, who was already seventy years old when he began painting 'for company' after his wife died. He did not think of his paintings as works of art, had no knowledge of the history of art, and there are even some indications that he used his paintings as a kind of magic to conjure up visions of his past. He was discovered by the painters Ben Nicholson and Christopher Wood when they happened to walk past his cottage in St Ives in Cornwall in 1928. They bought his paintings, which were on irregular pieces of cardboard, painted with house paint, recognising in them a beauty and naïvety which they were trying to achieve by a more sophisticated route. Admired by many of the most important artists and critics of the 1930s, Wallis's paintings were a major influence on a number of painters and were widely collected. Most commentators take it as obvious that they are works of art in their own right. Naum Gabo sent a wreath to Wallis's funeral which included the comment that Wallis was 'an artist without knowing it'.[14]

Dickie's Institutional Theory does not seem to allow the possibility of such outsider art being art in its own right. He would presumably treat Wallis's paintings as only becoming art at the point where Ben Nicholson and Christopher Wood, as members of the artworld, conferred that status upon them, whereas it seems

plausible to maintain that, as Gabo declared, Wallis was an artist without being aware that he was. The only way that Dickie could allow that Wallis's work was art before it was seen by Nicholson and Wood would be to recognise Wallis as a member of the artworld capable of conferring the status of work of art upon his own paintings. But that would seriously distort the nature of Wallis's activity, since it is clear that he did not see himself as part of any such institutional activity and operated outside it. It is even debatable whether – prior to being discovered – he even thought of his works as 'candidates for appreciation'.

Although Dickie's theory does not seem to deal adequately with cases such as that of Alfred Wallis, it does help to illuminate the way that some outsider art has achieved recognition as art. For instance, consider the case of the photographer E. J. Bellocq. Bellocq was a commercial photographer working in the early part of the twentieth century in Storyville in New Orleans. Little is known of his life, apart from the fact that he made a remarkable series of photographs of prostitutes, probably in 1912. A stash of his damaged glass negatives was discovered in his house after his death in 1949. These found their way into the possession of an established New York photographer, Lee Friedlander, who printed the negatives and exhibited 34 of them in the New York Museum of Modern Art. They were immediately hailed as significant works of photographic art. Bellocq was discussed as a naïve genius who had unwittingly achieved a new approach to the nude. Janet Malcolm has summed up the reaction:

Storyville, plate 33 (*c*.1912), E. J. Bellocq, © Lee Friedlander, courtesy of Fraenkel Gallery, San Francisco

Although the issue of 'the male gaze' – the unpleasant way in which male artists have traditionally scrutinized women's bodies as they painted or sculpted or photographed them – had not yet been raised as such, the friendliness of Bellocq's eye, the reciprocity that flowed between him and his subjects, could not but forcibly strike the viewer.[15]

Many of the features that made these photographs interesting to the New York art world were not deliberately chosen by the photographer. For example, part of their interest lies in the way in which the prostitutes are shown relaxed in their rooms. There are, however, many indications that Bellocq intended to block out the background when printing the images, and to present them as vignetted portraits. The photographic historian Steven Maklansky has demonstrated that, far from being a radical innovator in photography, Bellocq was almost certainly working within the pictorialist aesthetic of his time;[16] there is evidence that Bellocq never intended to print the full plates of the negatives, but instead would have printed these as oval vignettes, cropping out most of the elements that the art critics so praised. Furthermore, the cracks in the glass negatives, and the various erasures and scratches added by a later hand, add to the interest of the printed images (see, for example, p. 104). Janet Malcolm points out how these defacing marks make some of the photographs look like contributions to late twentieth-century art:

The pictures with the scratched-out faces have a high-art appearance that was surely not intended by the defacer but that developments in art have, willy-nilly, bestowed on them. The scribble – with its associations of aggression, negation, cancellation as well as of authenticity,

Schooner under the Moon (c.1935–6), Alfred Wallis, courtesy of Tate, London 2002

energy, individuality – is an established mannerism of contemporary art. (Cy Twombly, Pat Steir, Joseph Beuys, David Salle are some leading practitioners).[17]

Dickie's Institutional Theory can explain very well what happened in this case. Bellocq's photographs can plausibly be said to have the status of found art. He was working outside any understanding of his photography as artistic, and many of the elements now praised in his work were accidental rather than chosen and only have significance because of subsequent developments in modernist and postmodernist art. However, Friedlander saw features in the negatives which could justify his presenting them as candidates for appreciation to a wider public. This he did by organising the exhibition mentioned above. So Friedlander as a member of the artworld conferred the status of candidates for appreciation, and not the photographer.

Dickie's Institutional Theory was a return to traditional theorising about art. It set out necessary and sufficient conditions for something's being a work of art. Yet, despite the worries that Weitz and other neo-Wittgensteinians expressed about the foreclosing on creativity that would result from any traditional definition, Dickie's approach does not obviously impose cramping conditions on what can be art. Indeed, one of the most frequent criticisms of it is that it admits too much into the category of art, not too little.

The usual way in which Dickie's theory is attacked is for an art lover to complain that the theory trivialises art. For example, it has the consequence that an artist could exhibit a copy of the book you are currently reading in a glass case in the Art Institute of Chicago or Tate Modern and that would then be a work of art. Such an objection will only work if the art lover's intuitions about this are shared by the people he or she is trying to convince. For some people it is far from absurd to suggest that a copy of this book placed in a glass case in a gallery could be a work of art. The difficulty with this sort of criticism is that one person's absurdity is another person's common sense. Short of there being a visible contradiction, there are no rules for determining what is to count as an absurd consequence of a theory. Many adherents of the Institutional Theory will be happy to accept that, were this copy of this book treated in the way described, it would be transformed into a work of art, although not necessarily a particularly interesting or profound one. For those who firmly believe that such an eventuality would indeed be absurd, this is a telling indictment of the Institutional Theory, but it does not conclusively refute it.

A more sophisticated criticism of Dickie's theory attacks the assumptions it makes about the conferral of status carried out by members of the art world.[18] Either the members of the artworld confer the status of artwork for some reason or reasons, or else they do it in a completely whimsical and arbitrary way. If they do it for some reason or reasons, then presumably, if the reasons were spelt out, they would constitute a theory of what makes something a work of art, and that theory wouldn't be the Institutional Theory. For example, if the reasons that the art world confers the status of artwork on Hirst's *The Physical Impossibility of Death in the Mind of Someone Living* is that it deals with central human themes in a physical medium and is worthy of contemplation, then these reasons, together with others, might be shaped into a theory about why something has the status of artwork conferred. Clearly Dickie would be unwilling to accept that there could be a set of such reasons, since it would undermine his definition of what makes something a work of art being its having had the status of candidate for appreciation conferred upon it.

The other option offered in this sort of criticism is that the art world may confer the status of artwork on artifacts in an entirely whimsical and arbitrary way. This does seem consistent with Dickie's account. He does not want to lay down limits on when the status can appropriately be conferred, apart from the unlimiting element of his definition that makes artifactuality a necessary condition of something's being a work of art. But then the question is, surely, why should we be interested in what art is if it is produced by such a whimsical process? If the artworld has no good reason for making one thing rather than another a candidate for appreciation, then it is not at all clear why works of art have played so central a role in our culture.

A further criticism of Dickie's theory is that it is uninformative because of a circularity in its definition. His key concepts of 'artwork' and 'artworld' are defined each in terms of the other. An artwork is an artifact on which the artworld has conferred status; and the artworld is the group of people who have the power to confer the status of artwork. Dickie was well aware that his definition was circular. He did not see this as a serious objection, however, since the circularity is not vicious circularity. It is only when the circle of definition is so tight that there is no explanation involved that a definition can be damned for vicious circularity. He believes he says enough about what the artworld is and how it operates independently of his account of artworks for his definition not to be viciously circular. But even if it were viciously circular this would not prove that it was false. All it would show was that it was spectacularly uninformative about the very point on which we desire enlightenment.

There are, however, more obviously absurd consequences which follow from Dickie's theory, and serve to undermine it. For example, suppose that an established artist who is unquestionably a member of the artworld declared that every object ever produced in the history of humanity, and every object that ever will be produced, is art. That declaration would, on Dickie's theory confer the appropriate status of candidate for appreciation on every artifact. So the world would, at a stroke, become filled with works of art, whether or not we realised it. Indeed, this may already have happened without our knowing it. The artist could go even further and confer artifactuality on every aspect of the living world or even on the entire category of physical objects. Then the artist could expand his or her *oeuvre* to cover everything that we could possibly experience. The only obvious way out of this absurd consequence of the theory would be to allow that de-conferral as well as conferral of art status can take place. But this brings with it its own absurdities. Imagine a group of anti-artists who have the power of de-conferring status, declaring that all the objects currently exhibited in galleries are no longer art. Would that mean that the artworld would then have to re-declare them art, and start an escalating art/non-art war? The thought of objects flickering between art and non-art status is so far from most people's intuitions on what art is as to suggest that there is something seriously wrong with a theory that would apparently allow this consequence.

Recognising some of the inadequacies of his first version of the Institutional Theory, Dickie later presented a more elaborate definition. It consists of five interrelated definitions.

The main definition of art is:

A work of art is an artifact of a kind created to be presented to an artworld public.

This is supplemented by the following four definitions:

An artist is a person who participates with understanding in the making of a work of art.

A public is a set of persons the members of which are prepared in some degree to understand an object which is presented to them.

The artworld is the totality of all artworld systems.

> An artworld system is a framework for the presentation of a work of art by an artist to an artworld public.[19]

This definition loses the elegance and simplicity of the earlier one. Yet, like the previous formulation, it doesn't really address the question that people who ask 'What is art?' or 'But is it art?' really want answered.

The contemporary philosopher Jerrold Levinson has recently suggested an alternative to the Institutional Theory of art. His is usually known as a historical definition, or 'defining art historically', although this can be misleading. It is perhaps better described as an intentional–historical definition. Like the Institutional Theory, Levinson's theory attempts to give a definition broad enough to capture everything that is uncontroversially a work of art; like Dickie's theory, Levinson's does this by defining art in terms of the non-exhibited properties that all works of art share. He accepts Morris Weitz's insight that large-scale theorising of the past has been obviously hampered by the immense diversity of works of art. To find a single essential exhibited property common to the Wilton Diptych, Wallinger's *A Real Work of Art*, a painting by Wallis and a photograph by Cindy Sherman is no easy task. It may be an impossible one. Nevertheless, Levinson rejects the move of declaring that 'art' is a family resemblance term with no common denominator. In this respect, too, his theory is like Dickie's. But where Dickie's Institutional Theory concentrates on a procedure carried out by membership of the social institution he labels the artworld, Levinson's emphasises the intentions of those who create art.

Here is his definition in its simplest form:

> an artwork is a thing (item, object, entity) that has been seriously
> intended for regard-as-a-work-of-art – i.e. regard in any way pre-
> existing artworks are or were correctly regarded.[20]

This combines the insights that to produce a work of art requires
a particular kind of intention and that works of art have a special
sort of relation to the present and past practices of artists and
viewers. An object is, then, only a work of art if it has seriously
been intended to be treated as such. Furthermore, you can't turn
anything whatsoever into a work of art. Levinson has added the
stipulation that in order to make something a work of art you
must have a proprietary right over it; that is, you must either own
it yourself or have a right to use it in this way. I can't turn
every artifact in London into a work of art simply by intending
that every artifact in London be regarded as artworks of the past
have been regarded. That is because I don't have the appropriate
proprietorial right over all the artifacts in London. I can turn some
paint and canvas that I've bought into a work of art because I own
the raw materials. I can also produce commissioned works of art for
clients even if, strictly speaking, they own the raw materials from
which I make the works. But where someone else has appropriate
proprietorial rights over the materials I cannot simply override this
fact. Here is an obvious difference from Dickie's theory according
to which, if I am a member of the artworld, I will be able to confer
the status of artwork on any artifact whatsoever, whether or not
I happen to own it. If, in the course of a lecture – to make a point
about readymades – I suggest that the lectern in front of me has, in
the course of the lecture, been transformed into a work of art, this
again would not make it true that the lectern was a work of art.
Even though I might have intended my audience to view the lectern

in the ways that works of art of the past have been viewed for the course of the lecture, this would not constitute a 'serious', or as he puts it elsewhere a 'non-passing', intention to have it so regarded.

This condition of proprietorial right might seem to pose problems for conceptual artists. Take, for example, Richard Long's work *A Line Made by Walking, England*. In 1967, Long walked back and forth repeatedly over part of a park until the grass lay trampled flat. He documented the result – a temporary straight path through the grass – in a photograph. Long did not have any proprietary rights over the park, so it might seem that on Levinson's theory this could not be art. In fact Levinson would allow that such conceptual art is art even though it involves parts of the world not owned by the artist:

> One must just avoid the mistake of taking the art object in such cases to be simply and solely what the artist has described or pointed to (e.g. Marilyn Monroe, the Empire State Building, a slice of the life of a family in Queens – things that the artist clearly has no proprietary right over), rather than a directed complex of the description and object.[21]

Yet this is a transparent *ad hoc* move – every case in which a supposed artist uses something over which he or she has no proprietorial right in their art can be redescribed as 'a directed complex of the description and object', and so the proprietorial condition has no force whatsoever.

We have already considered some of the problems posed for the Institutional Theory of art by outsiders such as Alfred Wallis and E. J. Bellocq, artists apparently working beyond any context that could be described as an art world. These outsider artists differ, for example, from those psychiatric patients who before their mental breakdowns have been involved in the art world. Unlike, for example, Richard Dadd (1817–86), famous for his paintings of fairies, who spent most of his life in Bethlem Hospital and Broadmoor, Alfred Wallis and E. J. Bellocq worked entirely outside the art world. Dadd was established as one of the most talented artists of his generation before, believing that he was being persecuted by the devil and that his actions were controlled by the Egyptian god Osiris, he murdered his father. Despite being outside anything that could plausibly be described as an art world, at least until they were discovered, Wallis and Bellocq were in most people's estimation artists. The Institutional Theory of art fails to capture this intuition, as we have seen.

In contrast, Levinson's intentional–historical theory explains how the work of genuine outsider artists can also be art. Levinson allows several ways in which intentions can legitimately function in making something a work of art. First, an artist might intend his or her work to be regarded as a work of art (i.e. in some of the ways art of the past has been regarded). This can involve either a specific intention, such as that a wire sculpture can be viewed as wire sculptures in the past have been viewed. Or else it can involve a non-specific intention: the artist just wants it to be regarded in some of the ways art of the past has been regarded, without having a specific intention about which ways. However, the third kind of artistic intention that Levinson allows is the most relevant to the outsider-art case. He maintains that what he calls 'art-unconscious' intentions can suffice to make something a work of art. An artist such as Wallis, who no doubt wanted his paintings to be regarded as representations of ships at sea, could count as an artist even though he might be entirely ignorant of the fact that this is one of the ways in which art of the past has been regarded. As Levinson puts it:

> Such persons can be seen to make art if they intend their objects for regard in the ways that *happen to be*, unbeknown to them, in the repertory of aesthetic regards established at that time. In such a case there is the requisite link to the prior history of art, but it is one such art makers are unaware of, though they have in fact forged it.[22]

In this respect, then, Levinson's theory fits more closely with widespread intuitions about outsider art than does Dickie's Institutional Theory. Furthermore, with its emphasis on artists' intentions, history and art's evolutionary nature, it incorporates most of the features that seem intuitively important to art practice. Nevertheless, like all the philosophical theories examined in this book, it is open to a number of powerful criticisms.

First, the definition relies on the notion of there being appropriate past ways of regarding works of art. If we allow that what makes something a work of art is its relation to earlier art, then we have a problem when we get back to the very first art. There must have been some first work of art at some point in pre-history, yet what made this first art art rather than something else cannot have been that it was related in an appropriate way to the art that preceded it. There simply was no art that preceded it. Levinson is aware of this problem, and has given an account of what he calls Ur-art (after Ur, the first city) to explain what might have happened.

Levinson gives a complex account of Ur-art, which, like his account of how conceptual art involving objects over which artists do not have appropriate proprietorial rights, sounds suspiciously like special pleading. Even if we are prepared to accept it, there are further and more serious problems with his attempt at definition. It is true that his theory can accommodate any conceivable work of art, since it is impossible to imagine any new art so radical that it was not intended to be viewed in some of the ways art of the past had been appropriately regarded. Levinson's theory can easily cope with the 'anxious objects' discussed in this book, such as Mark Wallinger's *A Real Work of Art* or Tracey Emin's *My Bed*. Perhaps, then, Levinson has identified a necessary condition of something's being a work of art. However, the theory is over-inclusive.[23]

Take the case of looking at portraits. One of the appropriate ways of looking at art of the past has surely been to see more or less what sitters for portraits looked like. There is a long tradition of painted portraiture, and much of it goes far beyond the concern with appearances. Yet concern with verisimilitude has been an important aspect of portraiture. When looking at Alan Ramsay's famous portrait of the philosopher David Hume (see p. 28), for example, we get the best visual evidence we have of this individual's appearance, and regarding the portrait in this way must be allowed to be an appropriate regard in Levinson's sense. Certainly this is how most of Hume's contemporaries viewed the painting. King George III even commented on the fact that it made Hume look better-dressed than was his wont. The problem is that the makers of passport photographs and identikit pictures intend their work to be regarded in just this way, and yet are not obvious candidates for being considered works of art, at least not in most cases. One way that Levinson could easily avoid this consequence would be to deny that looking at portraits in order to see what someone looks like is an appropriate way of looking at works of art. But this would be highly counter-intuitive. Furthermore, the example I have given is only one of many cases in which objects that are not works of art seem to fulfil Levinson's criteria for something's being a work of art.

Promising as the intentional–historical theory appears in many respects, like the other attempts to define art we have examined, it appears flawed. This is the pessimistic conclusion of this book: all recent major philosophical attempts at defining art have been inadequate to some extent. No one has yet come up with a convincing account of what art is. In the final short chapter I put forward a hypothesis about where that leaves us.

Chapter Five | So What?

So far in this book I've examined a range of philosophical attempts to define art. These have included Clive Bell's formalism, R. G. Collingwood's expressionism, Wittgensteinian denials of the possibility of definition, George Dickie's Institutional Theory and Jerrold Levinson's intentional–historical definitions. All of these theories are flawed to some extent. Where does that leave us?

The most plausible hypothesis is that 'art' is indefinable not just at the exhibited level, but at the relational non-exhibited level, too. There is no simple argument that will lead irresistibly to this conclusion, but the inadequacies of a range of existing definitions, together with the ever-changing nature of art, make this conclusion likely. Maurice Mandelbaum suggested that there might be a common essential feature shared by all works of art that would not be the kind of feature that you might discern just with the eye.

Tiananmen Square, 4th June, 1989, Stuart Franklin, © Stuart Franklin/Magnum Photos

But the outcome of our investigation is that there is probably no such relational feature, or at least not one that will be particularly informative or interesting for us. It is very likely that art is a family resemblance term that will always defy attempts to pin it down in a definition. Notice that this is a more tentative conclusion than Weitz's. He thought it a logical mistake to look for the essence of art. My hypothesis is that 'art' is indefinable on the grounds that this is the most plausible position given the evidence.

It's not just that we can't see or imagine any important similarity between Leonardo da Vinci's cartoon in the National Gallery in London, Mark Wallinger's *A Real Work of Art* and a 'Film Still' photograph by Cindy Sherman. It's that the three share no common defining feature at all, but rather are related by a pattern of culturally significant overlapping resemblances. We can use the term 'art' effectively and understand each other when we talk about art, but that is not because all works of art have some defining essential ingredient that makes art what it is. We have culturally determined patterns and tacit agreements about relevant resemblances that can justify our expanding the concept of art to cover new cases. Different sub-cultures draw the lines in different places. There is no ingredient X for the would-be art-definer to seize upon. Nothing that will explain the use of the term 'art' beyond the fact that, culturally, various groups have made certain decisions about what is to count as a relevant resemblance between a new object and paradigm cases of art. Often the decision-makers act arbitrarily. Some individuals and groups of people have disproportionate power over how decisions are made about difficult cases. And some groups have vested interests in drawing the line in one place rather than another: this is particularly obvious in the art world where the label 'art' immediately raises the price of an artifact.

We are now in a position to step back and examine the question, What is the point of a definition? Why do we want or need a definition at all? It is easy to get absorbed in the minutiae of the philosophical definition-spinning and at the same time lose sight of the point of the whole enterprise. Here are three possible uses of a definition of art:

1   To help us decide difficult cases
2   To explain retrospectively why what has been called art is art
3   To tell us which objects in the world are likely to repay specific kinds of close attention

1 To help us decide difficult cases

When confronted with the 'anxious objects' of the sorts mentioned throughout this book – such as Duchamp's readymades, Warhol's *Brillo Box* or more recent works such as Emin's *My Bed* – a clear definition of art might help us decide whether these so-called works of art genuinely deserve that name. Take an unusual installation shown in the Serpentine Gallery in London in 2000: *Untitled (Placebo) 1991* by the Cuban artist Felix Gonzales-Torres (described in *The Independent*, 20 May 2000). This consisted of 1,200 lb of Cellophane-wrapped caramel chocolates bought from a chain store and spread across the floor of the gallery. Visitors were encouraged to eat the chocolates, which were replenished each day. This work immediately and predictably triggered the 'But is it art?' question for many of those who heard about or visited the installation. A satisfactory definition of art should tell us whether this was just confectionery, or whether it really was a work of art. It might go beyond this categorisation issue and explain to us what it is about the work which justifies anyone calling it art. It might even suggest ways in which to approach and understand the work as in some way a contribution to our culture and something worth trying to understand.

2 To explain retrospectively why what has been called art is art

When people ask 'But is it art?' they usually do so because they suspect that the answer is 'No'. Some theories of art, however, don't allow that artists and museum curators could ever make a mistake about art. Instead, as George Dickie does, they begin from facts about the world of art and its associated institutions and work back from these to an explanation. The behaviour of artists, art markets, gallery owners and museum curators is for this sort of theorist the raw data. The philosopher comes in at a later stage to try to make sense of what has happened. Typically when a philosopher who takes this approach to definitions of art asks 'But is it art?' they will answer 'Yes'.

Such an approach to the art question is only sustainable if you believe that 'art' is a neutral term that need have no moral or other evaluative connections. If, however, you believe that to call something 'art' implies that that object has value and perhaps is of a kind that sets it apart from more mundane objects, then to take the practices of the art world as your starting-point is a risky strategy. That's like investigating the meaning of 'justice' by examining how different cultures (including Nazi Germany) have used the term and seeking some common essence that explains the use.

3 To tell us which objects in the world are likely to repay specific kinds of close attention

Some people, when they ask the art question, are not seeking an explanation of why difficult objects might be considered art. Nor do they want to discover some sort of retrospective justification for the behaviour of the art world. Instead, asking what is art is an indirect way of asking questions about which objects in the world are likely to repay certain sorts of attention. On this view 'art' is quite clearly an evaluative term. It is also a term with moral implications. Life is short, and each of us must decide how we spend it, assuming that we have a choice. The point of answering the art question, then, is to communicate to others enriching and fulfilling ways of using our time. Thus, for Bell and for Collingwood, it was obvious that art had moral implications. Defining art was not a technical exercise to pass the time or bolster a career. The answer to the question 'What is art?' really mattered to these two thinkers because both saw that art could play a central role in a worthwhile life.

The first sort of use of a definition when taken in isolation is a relatively trivial one. If the objects we are categorising don't have particular significance or value for us, then it doesn't really matter if we struggle when we try to put them into two categories: art and non-art. It is a trivial question as to whether Tracey Emin's *My Bed* is art or not if the category 'art' is not an evaluative one. If philosophers of art just end up rationalising the arbitrary decisions made by members of the art world, then that is also an imaginative but ultimately unrewarding enterprise. Answering the question about why some people have used the word 'art' in certain ways, applying it to some cases but not others, is probably of most interest to anthropologists. If, however, asking the art question helps us to focus on which objects might repay certain sorts of attention, and suggests how we might fruitfully approach them, then it can still have some point. My hypothesis is that this third sense of the art question is still worth asking but is best asked of individual works rather than as a general question.

Even though 'art' is probably indefinable, we can usefully discuss particular questions. We should probably stop wasting our time on the pursuit of some all-encompassing definition – there are better ways of spending a life, and the pursuit is almost certainly a futile one. Yet we can fruitfully examine and compare particular works and bring out in those cases what it is that makes one or other of them art and why it matters. The situation is analogous to the judgements we make about the value of particular works of art. We might want to say that what makes Francis Bacon's paintings profound is their direct engagement with the darker elements of the human psyche. Yet it does not follow from this that any painter who engages directly with the darker elements of the human psyche will therefore be a significant artist. Nor, indeed, that a painter who engages directly with the darker elements of the human psyche will inevitably be superior to one who is concerned with lighter themes. It is not obvious that Chardin or Cézanne, for instance, is inferior to Bacon as an artist. Making the particular judgement in the particular case does not commit us to the general rule. Indeed, the general rule would be obviously absurd.

I want to end this book with an illustration of my hypothesis – that the role of theorising about art's definition is best restricted to particular cases and that in these cases it is often an indirect way of investigating how best we should approach individual works. Compare two photographs, one a 'Film Still' by Cindy Sherman, the other a photograph of a student standing in front of a tank in Tiananmen Square in 1989, photographed by Stuart Franklin.

Cindy Sherman is a photographer who has always seen herself as an artist rather than simply a photographer:

> The only reason I don't call myself a photographer is that I don't think other people who consider themselves photographers would think I'm one of them.[1]

She uses photography as her artistic medium and, usually, herself as a model. The photograph I want to consider, *Untitled Film Still #21*, is a self-portrait taken in 1978 (see p. 128). It is part of the Film Stills series, a black and white series alluding to the genre of still photographs used to advertise movies. These Film Stills are all self-portraits, with Sherman taking the lead role, and no other actors in shot (apart from number 7, in which another character features wearing a straw hat, and number 65, in which there is a stranger lurking in the shadows). They are printed in 10 inch by 8 inch format, in emulation of the original proportions and size of film stills. Sherman deliberately copied the grainy, slightly out-of-focus style of original film stills. Like the rest of the series, which runs to approximately 80 images, *Untitled Film Still #21* is a product of her

Untitled Film Still #21 (1978), Cindy Sherman, courtesy the artist and Metro Pictures

imagination, and not based on any particular real film. Sherman takes on a role that an actress might have played, but didn't. In the process she explores an implied narrative. For some commentators, such as the philosopher and art critic Arthur Danto, the images in the Film Still series embody metaphors for the meaning of our existence. They transcend the particular and express something profound about life:

> I can think of no body of work at once so timeless and yet so much of its own time as Cindy Sherman's stills, no oeuvre which addresses us in our common humanity and at the same time induces the most advanced speculations on Post-Modernity, no images which say

something profound about the feminine condition and yet touch us at a level beyond sexual difference. They are wry, arch, clever works, smart, sharp, and cool. But they are among the rare works of recent decades that rise to the demand on great art, that it embody the transformative metaphors for the meaning of human reality.[2]

Whether or not you agree with the judgement that Sherman's images have the status of great art, they are undoubtedly works of art at some level. Yet what is it that makes them such? One element is the use of a series of images to express complex and subtle ideas. Although the photographer is in a sense present as the model for the photographs, it is her presence as shaping personality behind the photographs that is more forceful in this series. There is an implied photographer, a shaping intellect behind the concept of the series, which plays with a banal genre and turns it into a powerful medium for expression.[3] We know that these images are not film stills; yet they have all the appearance of being just that. The photographer communicates through the subversion of the genre. She draws attention to her own choices through the presentation of these images in exhibitions and books. We couldn't mistake them for actual film stills, given these contexts of presentation. Instead we must ask ourselves what it is that she is expressing through this choice of genre. Much of what is distinctive and original in this series is not given to us visually. The conceptual framework implied by the contexts of presentation communicates a more complex and more interesting meaning than would ever be open to actual film stills, even if such film stills were visually indistinguishable from Sherman's photographs.

What makes Sherman's photographs works of art is not, almost paradoxically, their appearance, but the way in which they function in relation to their context of presentation, the sorts of idea which they can express through this relation to context (and to the photographer and her known output). The relation between individual photographs and the larger series is also important in interpreting the meaning of individual images. It is this which allows us to discern what is accidental and what chosen, which aspects of the particular image are of especial concern to the photographer, and so on. Recognising that Sherman's photographs can function and be interpreted in this way suggests how we as viewers can approach and appreciate them. This is an aspect of recognising that they are works of art. Cynics might also note that, like many photographic artists, she makes limited editions of her prints, a device that plays to the art market's desire to guarantee rarity of works of art and thus increase the price of potentially reproducible images.

None of the features of Sherman's work mentioned is generalisable in a straightforward way – we won't answer the larger question 'What is art?' by thinking about her photographs, but we might come to understand her photographs better by thinking about what makes them works of art and how that affects our understanding of them.

Contrast this with Stuart Franklin's famous image taken during the student pro-democracy protests in Beijing's Tiananmen Square in 1989 (see p. 120). Chinese troops had arrived to crush the students' protests. As no one was allowed on the street, Franklin photographed the scene from a hotel balcony overlooking Tiananmen Square. He describes what happened:

> We could see a bit of Tiananmen Avenue very clearly and we could
> see the army had taken over the square completely. I photographed

what I could. I had already seen students being dispersed by soldiers, then the tanks began to move out of the square and a young man from the hotel side of the road suddenly jumped out in front of them and started a conversation with the tank driver and then climbed on top of the tank. Then some friends or colleagues came out from the side of the road and pulled him away and he disappeared in the crowd and the tanks moved off. All this happened within a few minutes. I had no sense of this being an important picture.[4]

This student's bravery and defiance were also filmed, and the images widely shown on television. Franklin's still image of the student facing up to a line of tanks records a moment that symbolises non-violent resistance, the tiny figure of the unarmed student stopping, albeit for a few minutes, the apparently relentless progress of the tanks. Like most great photojournalistic images, this photograph records a significant instant that takes on a much wider symbolic significance. Thus, for example, Robert Capa's famous image of a Spanish Republican soldier at the very instant of his death has come to symbolise not just one person's death (if, indeed, it does record that), but Republican Spain bravely taking on the fascists and, at the universal level, death in war. Franklin's photograph transcends the particular moment, which was the reason for his taking it, and it has already come to represent heroic defiance of oppression, beyond the context of the Chinese authorities' suppression of the pro-democracy movement.

There is nothing in the appearance of the photograph, nor in its symbolic functioning, to preclude its being a work of art. Yet that is not, currently, what it is. Even though fine prints of this image are sold by the art market, its current status is not a work of photographic art, but a remarkable journalistic photograph. In the future it may function as a work of art and be widely accorded the sorts of aesthetic and artistic scrutiny accorded to the work of Cindy Sherman. At that point, viewers may pay more attention to the relationship between this image and other images made by Franklin, to formal aspects of the composition, and so on. But that has not yet happened. This is not in any way to denigrate the image. Far from it. It has a greater value to humanity than most (some might argue all) artistic photographs. It records in a memorable form an event, transforming it into a symbol for non-violent protest and defiance. But, at this short distance from the event it records, to treat it in some of the ways that artworks are traditionally treated would risk aestheticising the event.

Cindy Sherman's *Untitled Film Still #21* invites questions about role-playing, the nature of the self, and the ironic use of popular genres. In contrast, Stuart Franklin's photograph is not self-reflective and invites questions about the subject matter, not so much about the photographer's intentions: in the great tradition of photojournalism it is about the events unfolding in front of the lens. Franklin used the camera as a sophisticated recording instrument, not so as to draw attention to an artist's interpretation of events, but to provide documentary evidence of oppression and resistance.

Yet we cannot conclude from this that any photograph that is self-reflective, ironic and reflects attention to the photographer is necessarily a work of art; nor that photojournalism is incompatible with art photography. It would be easy to provide a range of counter-examples to each of these generalisations. That is the point. The art question resists just this sort of general claim. We can assess the aspects of Cindy Sherman's photograph that justify our discussing it as a work of art. Yet turning these aspects into rules will not give us a reliable indication of what makes something a work of photographic art. We can recognise the way in which Stuart Franklin's photograph is a contribution to photojournalism and not to art, but cannot spell out precisely the conditions under which photojournalism becomes art, nor rule out the possibility that at some time it will become art. All this requires attention to the particular case and not the formulation of general rules.

Conclusion

The art question, when asked at the general level of 'What is art?', is probably not answerable. Given the brevity of life, if we are going to ask the question at all, it is better to focus on the particular works and ask of them why they are art and why this might matter to us. Those philosophers drawn to the crossword-puzzle-like technicalities of coming up with a watertight yet general answer to the question 'What is art?' should be left to their own devices. For most of us, the rewarding questions in this area will be the questions that touch real works of art. This is nothing to be embarrassed about. The whole point of the art question is that it is asked by people interested in works of art, not simply in the idea of art. Ultimately we must turn back to the works themselves.

Notes

Introduction   Art and Philosophy

1 Quoted in 'Portrait of the Artist as a Young Peacock', *The Times*, 6 June 2001, p.1.
2 Quoted in Tomkins, p.182.
3 Quoted in Tomkins, p.185.

Chapter One   Significant Form

1 Bell, p. 25.
2 Bell, p. 27.
3 This is the title Bell gives it, but its official title is *The Railway Station* 1862. For further information about this painting, see *Art Treasures of England*, pp. 220–1.
4 Bell, p. 18.
5 Waugh, p. 30.
6 Bell, p. 59.
7 Bell, p. 60.
8 Bell, p. 61.
9 Bell, p. 62.
10 Bell, p. 37.
11 Bell, p. 44.
12 Cézanne, quoted in Farr, p. 92.
13 Bell, pp. 7–8.
14 Lawrence, pp. 324–5.
15 Lawrence, p. 331.
16 Lawrence, p. 341.
17 Berger, p. 13.
18 Berger, p. 13.
19 Berger, p. 15.
20 See Rawls

Chapter Two   Expression of Emotion

1 Collingwood (1958), p. 114.
2 Bell, p. 37.
3 For an interesting discussion of the evolution of the concept of fine art, see Kristeller.
4 Collingwood (1958), p. vi.
5 Collingwood (1978), p. 2.
6 By Simon Blackburn in his entry on Collingwood in the *Routledge Encyclopedia of Philosophy*, p. 414. Despite this praise, the book is given only brief and superficial treatment in the article – perhaps a symptom of the relative importance assigned to the philosophy of art in the analytic philosophy tradition.
7 Collingwood (1958), p. 1.
8 Collingwood (1958), pp. 15–16.
9 Quoted in Herbert Read, *Art Now*, p. 123 (see Gale, p. 71).
10 Collingwood (1958), p. 26.
11 Quoted in Pevsner (1960), p. 23.
12 Quoted in Pevsner (1960), p. 23.
13 Quoted in Pevsner (1960) p. 25.
14 Collingwood (1958) p. 26.
15 Sheppard, p. 28.
16 Sheppard, p. 28.
17 Collingwood (1958), p. 22.
18 Collingwood (1958), p. 22.
19 Wilkinson, p. 187.
20 Wilkinson, p. 187.
21 Collingwood (1958), p. 28.
22 Collingwood (1958), p. 21.
23 Sylvester, pp. 148–9.
24 Pacheco, p. 31.
25 Collingwood (1958), p. 114.
26 Collingwood (1958), p. 111.
27 Collingwood (195^), p. 109.
28 Collingwood (1958), p. 122.
29 Collingwood (1958), p. 308.
30 Collingwood (1958), p. 66.
31 Collingwood (1958), p. 78.
32 Collingwood (1958), p. 81.
33 Hitchock, quoted in Truffaut, p. 233.
34 See Hitchcock's comments to this effect in Truffaut, p. 236.
35 For example, Collingwood (1958), p.103. However, elsewhere in the book Collingwood seems to take for granted Shakespeare's status as an artist proper.
36 Collingwood (1958), p. 95.
37 Collingwood (1958), p. 130.
38 Collingwood (1958), p. 151.
39 Collingwood (1958), p. 147.
40 Collingwood (1958), p. 148.
41 Knox, p. 156.
42 Collingwood (1958), p. 72.
43 This has been demonstrated effectively by Neil MacGregor. See MacGregor, pp. 16–17.

Chapter Three   Family Resemblances

1 Malcolm (1958), pp. 51–2.
2 In his book *But Is It Art?*, Tilghman uses this same incident to make a related point about Wittgenstein's discussion of games. It's such a good example that I couldn't resist using it, too.

3   Bell, p. 7.
4   Wittgenstein, *Philosophical Investigations*, I, p. 66.
5   Quoted in Glock, p. 120.
6   Weitz, pp. 183–91.
7   Weitz, p. 184.
8   Weitz, p. 189.
9   Weitz, p. 189.
10   Godfrey, p. 19.
11   Weitz, p. 189.
12   Lessing, p. 75.
13   Burke, p. 29.
14   Burke, p. 29.
15   It is worth noting that Bell believes that his account of art applies to all art of the past, and presumably that of the future, too; Collingwood, in contrast, only purports to elucidate the art of his own time.
16   Weitz, p. 188.
17   Weitz, p. 184.
18   Weitz, p. 192.
19   Weitz, p. 192.
20   Weitz, p. 192.

Chapter Four Institutional Contexts

1   Davies (1991), especially pp. 23–47.
2   See Davies (1991), especially pp. 23–47.
3   Danto (1995), p. 205.
4   Danto (1995), p. 209. 'Descry' simply means 'catch sight of'.
5   Danto (1995), p. 210.
6   Danto (1981), p. 2.
7   Berger, pp. 27–8.
8   Berger, p. 28.
9   Dickie (1974), p. 34.
10   Dickie (*Introduction to Aesthetics*, 1997), p. 86.
11   Wolfe, p. 26.
12   Quoted in Ferrier, p. 12.
13   Quoted in Maizels, pp. 33–4.
14   Mentioned in Gale, p. 68.
15   Malcolm (1997), p. 12.
16   Malcolm (1997), pp. 14–15.
17   Malcolm (1997), p. 15.
18   This sort of criticism was made by Richard Wollheim.
19   Dickie (1997), p. 92.
20   Levinson, pp. 38–9.
21   Levinson, p. 10.
22   Levinson (1990), p. 11.
23   Noël Carroll (1999) argues this point persuasively.

Chapter Five So What?

1   Quoted in Morris, p. 12.
2   Arthur Danto (1990), p. 14.
3   For a discussion of the concept of style in photography, see Nigel Warburton.
4   Quoted in Miller, pp. 276–7.

Bibliography

Art Treasures of England – The Regional Collections, London: Royal Academy of Arts in association with Merrell Holberton, 1998.

Bell, Clive, *Art*, Oxford: Oxford University Press, 1987.

Berger, John, *Ways of Seeing*, London: BBC and Penguin, 1972.

Blackburn, Simon, 'R. G. Collingwood' in Craig (ed.) *Routledge Encyclopedia of Philosophy*, London and New York: Routledge, 1998.

Budd, Malcolm *Values of Art*, London: Penguin, 1996.

Burke, Edmund *A Philosophical Enquiry into the Origin of our Ideas of the Sublime and Beautiful*, Oxford: Oxford University Press, 1990.

Carroll, Noël, 'Clive Bell's aesthetic hypothesis', in Dickie, Sclafani and Roblin (eds) *Aesthetics: A Critical Anthology*, 2nd edn, New York: St Martin's Press, 1989.

Carroll, Noël, *Philosophy of Art: A Contemporary Introduction*, London: Routledge, 1999.

Carroll, Noël (ed.), *Theories of Art Today*, Madison, Wis.: University of Wisconsin Press, 2000 [contains a very useful bibliography].

Collingwood, R. G., *The Principles of Art*, Oxford: Oxford University Press, 1958.

Collingwood, R. G., *An Autobiography*, Oxford: Clarendon, 1978.

Craig, Edward (ed.), *Routledge Encyclopedia of Philosophy*, London and New York: Routledge, 1998.

Danto, Arthur, 'The Artworld', in Neill and Ridley (eds), *The Philosophy of Art: Readings Ancient and Modern*, New York: McGraw-Hill, 1995.

Danto, Arthur, *The Transfiguration of the Commonplace*, Cambridge, Mass.: Harvard University Press, 1981.

Danto, Arthur, 'Photography and performance: Cindy Sherman's stills', in *Sherman Untitled Film Stills*, London: Jonathan Cape, 1990.

Davies, Stephen, *Definitions of Art*, Ithaca, NY: Cornell University Press, 1991.

Davies, Stephen, 'Art, definitions of', in Edward Craig (ed.), *Routledge Encyclopedia of Philosophy*, London and New York: Routledge, 1998.

Dickie, George, *Art and the Aesthetic*, Ithaca, NY: Cornell University Press, 1974.

Dickie, George, *The Art Circle*, Evanston, Ill.: Chicago Spectrum Press, 1997.

Dickie, George, *Introduction to Aesthetics*, Oxford: Oxford University Press, 1997.

Dutton, Denis (ed.), *The Forger's Art*, Berkeley, Calif.: University of California Press, 1983.

Farr, Dennis (ed.), *100 Masterpieces from the Courtauld Collections: Bernardo Daddi to Ben Nicholson*, London: Courtauld Institute of Art Fund, 1987.

Ferrier, Jean-Louis, *Outsider Art*, Paris: Terrail, 1998.

Gale, Matthew, *Alfred Wallis*, London: Tate Gallery Publishing, 1998.

Glock, Hans-Johann, *A Wittgenstein Dictionary*, Oxford: Blackwell, 1996.

Godfrey, Tony, *Conceptual Art*, London: Phaidon, 1998.

Ground, Ian, *Art or Bunk?*, Bristol: Bristol Classical Press, 1989.

Hanfling, Oswald (ed.), *Philosophical Aesthetics*, Oxford: Blackwell and The Open University, 1992.

Harrison, Charles, *English Art and Modernism 1900–1939*, 2nd edn, New Haven, Conn. and London: Yale University Press, 1994.

Holborn, Mark, *Bellocq*, London: Jonathan Cape, 1996.

Johnson, Peter, *R. G. Collingwood: An Introduction*, Bristol: Thoemmes Press, 1998.

Knox, T. M., 'Collingwood, Robin George' in Colin Matthew (ed.), *Brief Lives*, Oxford: Oxford University Press, 1999.

Kristeller, Oscar, 'The modern system of the arts', in Peter Kivy (ed.), *Essays on the History of Aesthetics*, Rochester, NY: University of Rochester Press, 1992.

Lawrence, D.H., 'Introduction to his paintings', in *D. H. Lawrence Selected Essays*, Harmondsworth: Penguin, 1950.

Lessing, Alfred, 'What is wrong with a forgery?', in Denis Dutton (ed.) *The Forger's Art*, Berkeley, Calif.: University of California Press, 1983.

Levinson, Jerrold, *Music, Art and Metaphysics*, Ithaca, NY: Cornell University Press, 1990.

Lyas, Colin, *Aesthetics* London: UCL Press, 1997.

MacGregor, Neil with Langmuir, Erika, *Making Masterpieces*, London: BBC Education and National Gallery Publications, 1997.

Maizels, John, *Raw Creation: Outsider Art and Beyond*, London: Phaidon, 1996.

Malcolm, Janet, 'The Real Thing', in *Diana and Nikon*, expanded edn, New York: Aperture, 1997.

Malcolm, Norman, *Ludwig Wittgenstein: A Memoir*, Oxford: Oxford University Press, 1958.

Mandelbaum, Maurice, 'Family resemblances and generalizations concerning the arts' in Neill and Ridley (eds), *The Philosophy of Art: Readings Ancient and Modern*, New York: McGraw-Hill, 1995.

Miller, Russell, *Magnum*, London: Pimlico, 1999.

Moore, G.E., *Principia Ethica*, Cambridge: Cambridge University Press, 1903.

Morris, Catherine, *The Essential Cindy Sherman*, New York: Harry N. Abrams, 1999.

Neill, Alex and Ridley, Aaron (eds), *The Philosophy of Art: Readings Ancient and Modern*, New York: McGraw-Hill, 1995.

Neill, Alex and Ridley, Aaron (eds) *Arguing about Art*, 2nd edn, London: Routledge, 2002.

Pacheco, Ana Maria, *Ana Maria Pacheco at the National Gallery*, exhibition catalogue, London: National Gallery Publications, 1999.

Pevsner, Nikolaus, *Pioneers of Modern Design*, revised edn, London: Penguin, 1960.

Rawls, John, *A Theory of Justice*, revised edn, Oxford: Oxford University Press, 1999.

Ridley, Aaron, *R. G. Collingwood: A Philosophy of Art*, London: Phoenix, 1998.

Robins, Anna Gruetzner, *Modern Art in Britain 1910–1914*, London: Merrell Holberton and Barbican Art Gallery, 1997.

Rosenthal, Norman, *et al.*, *Sensation*, London: Thames & Hudson and Royal Academy of Arts, 1998.

Sheppard, Anne, *Aesthetics*, Oxford: Oxford University Press, 1987.

Sherman, Cindy, *Cindy Sherman Untitled Film Stills*, London: Jonathan Cape, 1990.

Stallabrass, Julian, *High Art Lite: British Art in the 90s*, London: Verso, 1999.

Stecker, Robert, *Artworks: Definition, Meaning and Value*, Pennsylvania: Pennsylvania State University Press, 1997.

Sylvester, David, *Interviews with Francis Bacon*, London: Thames & Hudson, 1993.

Szarkowski, John (ed.) *E. J. Bellocq: Storyville Portraits*, New York: Museum of Modern Art, 1970.

Tilghman, B. R., *But Is It Art?*, Oxford: Blackwell, 1984.

Tomkins, Calvin, *Duchamp: A Biography*, London: Chatto & Windus, 1997.

Truffaut, Franços, *Hitchcock*, London: Secker & Warburg, 1968.

Warburton, Nigel, 'Individual style in photographic art', *British Journal of Aesthetics*, in Neill and Ridley (eds), *Arguing about Art*, 2nd edn, London: Routledge, 2002.

Waugh, Evelyn, *Brideshead Revisited*, Harmondsworth: Penguin, 1962.

Weitz, Morris, 'The role of theory in aesthetics', in Neill and Ridley (eds), *The Philosophy of Art: Readings Ancient and Modern*, New York: McGraw-Hill, 1995.

Wilkinson, Robert, 'Art, Emotion and Expression', in Oswald Hanfling (ed.), *Philosophical Aesthetics*, Oxford: Blackwell and the Open University, 1992.

Wittgenstein, Ludwig, *Philosophical Investigations*, 3rd edn, Oxford: Blackwell, 1967.

Wolfe, Tom, *The Painted Word*, New York: Bantam Books, 1976.

Wollheim, Richard, 'The Institutional Theory of art', in *Art and Its Objects*, 2nd edn, Cambridge: Cambridge University Press, 1992.

Further Reading

General Anthologies

If you are interested in reading more about the philosophy of art generally, the two anthologies listed below are a good place to start:

Neill, Alex and Ridley, Aaron (eds) *The Philosophy of Art: Readings Ancient and Modern*, New York: McGraw-Hill, 1995.

Neill, Alex and Ridley, Aaron (eds) *Arguing about Art*, 2nd edn, London: Routledge, 2002.

Introductions to the Philosophy of Art

Noël Carroll, *Philosophy of Art: A Contemporary Introduction*, London: Routledge, 1999, is an interesting and wide-ranging introduction by a leading contributor to the debate on what art is.

If you are drawn to Collingwood's account of art, then you will probably enjoy Colin Lyas, *Aesthetics: An Introduction*, London: UCL Press, 1997.

Books on the Definition of Art

For detailed discussion of the range of recent attempts to answer the art question, see Stephen Davies, *The Definition of Art*, Ithaca, NY: Cornell University Press, 1991, and Noël Carroll (ed.), *Theories of Art Today*, Madison, Wis.: University of Wisconsin Press, 2000 (this also includes a useful bibliography of articles and books published in this area). B. R. Tilghman, *But Is It Art?*, Oxford: Blackwell, 1984, is also well worth reading.

Index

Figures in **bold** type refer to pages containing illustrations

Abstract Expressionism 76
aesthetic emotion 12–13,
    14–15, 19–20, 22,
    defined 23–4
Alys, Francis: *The
    Ambassador* 1–2, 3, 89
amusement art, *see*
    entertainment
anxious objects 2–3, 4, 117,
    123
art brut 102
art world 99–100, 101, 109,
    122, 126
artifact 96–7, 100–1, 110,
    122
Arts and Crafts movement
    41–2

Bacon, Francis 44–9, 126,
    127; *Figures at the Base
    of a Crucifixion* **45–7**;
    Passport Photos **44**
beauty 12–13
Bell, Clive: aesthetic emotion
    12–13, 14–15, 19–20,
    22, 23–4; *Art* **5**, 9–35, 37,
    38, 39, 57, 62, 68, 72,
    79, 83, 91, 95, 125;
    context 32–4; descriptive
    painting 11; elitism 24–5;
    formalism 121; imitation

13–14; metaphysical
    hypothesis 13; morality
    20; representation
    10–12, 18, 26, 27–9, 33;
    significant form 5, 10,
    22, 22, 37; timelessness
    15, 37; universality 15,
    37
Bellini, Giovanni: *Madonna of
    the Meadows* 65
Bellocq, E. J. 103, 105–8,
    114, 115; *Storyville* **104**,
    105
Berenson, Bernard 56
Berger, John: *Ways of Seeing*
    29–32, 94–5
Beuys, Josef 34, 107
Blind Man, The (magazine) 2
Bloomsbury set 19, 20
Borges, Jorge Luis 93
Brett, James 11
Burke, Edmund: *A
    Philosophical Enquiry* 78

Calvin, Jean 26
Capa, Robert 131
Cattelan, Maurizio:
    *Novecento (Twentieth
    century)* **86**, 89–90
Catullus 42–3
Cézanne, Paul 9, 15–16, 21,

22, 26–7, 38, 126–7; *Lac
    D'Annecy* 16–18, **17**, 56
Chardin, J.-B.-S. 126–7
Chartres cathedral 21
Collingwood, R. G.:
    amusement art 51–4; art
    and craft 39–44, 48, 49,
    61–2; art proper and
    so-called art 54–5, 57,
    61; *Autobiography*
    38–9; emotional
    expression 5;
    Expressionism 55,
    57–60, 121; Idealism 55;
    imagination 55–6;
    imaginative expression
    of emotion 49–50;
    language 57; magic
    art 51–2, 60; *The
    Principles of Art* 37–62,
    79, 83, 91, 95, 125;
    religious art 60–1; ritual
    51; technical theory of
    art 40–4
Collingwood, William 38
commissions 40–1
context 32–4, 90, 93, 94
copies 13–14, 77
craftwork 39–44, 48, 49,
    61–2
Crane, Walter 42

Croce, Benedetto 57

dadaism 35, 90
Dadd, Richard 115
Danto, Arthur: 'The artworld'
    91; 'Photography and
    performance' 128–9; *The
    Transfiguration of the
    Commonplace* 93
Davies, Stephen 90–1
defining art historically 5
Delphic oracle 4
descriptive painting 11
Dickie, George: artifact 96–7,
    110; artwork 99, 110,
    111; Institutional Theory
    5, 84–5, 90, 91, 95–118,
    121, 124; status 98, 99,
    100–1, 103, 109, 110
'difficult' paintings 16
Dos Passos, John: *U.S.A.* 80
Dubuffet, Jean 102
Duchamp, Marcel 34, 90;
    Fountain 2–3, 34–5, 74,
    88; readymades 2–3, 73,
    88–9, 123

Eliot, T. S. 38
Emin, Tracy: *My Bed* 73–4,
    75, 117, 123, 126
emotional expression 5,
    49–50
Empire State Building 81, 114
entertainment 51–4
Expressionism 55, 57–60,
    121

family resemblance 68, 72,
    82, 83–4, 122
film 52–4, **53**, 61–2, **128**
Flatow, Louis Victor 11
forgeries 13–14, 77
formalism 5, 29–32, 121
found art 90, 99
Franklin, Stuart: *Tiananmen
    Square, China* **120**, 127,
    130–3
Friedlander, Lee 105, 108
Frith, William Powell: *The
    Railway Station* **8**, 11–12,
    15
Fry, Roger 9
functional theory of art
    90–1

Gabo, Naum 103–5
games 66–71, 84
George III 117
Giacometti, Alberto: *Man
    Pointing* 65
Gide, Andre: *The School for
    Wives* 80, 81
Giotto 21, 22
Godfrey, Tony 73
Goethe, J. W. von 77
Gonzales-Torres, Felix:
    Untitled (Placebo) 1991
    123–4

Hals, Frans: *Regentesses of
    the Old Men's Alms
    House* 29, **30–1**
happenings 90
Haydn, Josef 77
Haydon, Michael 11
Hirst, Damien 22; *Mother and
    Child Divided* 80–1; *The
    Physical Impossibility of
    Death in the Mind of
    Someone Living* 87,
    88–9, 90, 100–1, 109; *A
    Thousand Years* 101
Hitchcock, Alfred: *Psycho*
    52–4, **53**, 61–2
Hodgkin, Howard 24, 98

Idealism 55
identikit pictures 117
imagination 55–6
imitation 13–14, 27, 77
Independent, The 123
insanity, *see* mental illness
inspiration 41
installations 123
Institutional Theory 5, 90, 91,
    95–118, 121, 124;
    defined 95, 111–12
intentional-historical definition
    112, 115–16, 118, 121
intuitionism 19

Johns, Jasper 65
Joyce, James: *Finnegans
    Wake* 80

Knox, T. M. 60

language 57, 66
Lawrence, D. H. 25–6

Leonardo da Vinci 77, 122
Lessing, Alfred 77
Levinson, Jerrold: intentional-
    historical definition
    112–14, 115–16, 118,
    121; Ur–art 116
Long, Richard: *A Line Made
    by Walking, England* 114

magic art 51–2, 60
Maklansky, Steven 106
Malcolm, Janet 105–7
Malcolm, Mr and Mrs Norman
    66–7, 70–1
Mandelbaum, Maurice 83–4,
    95, 121
Matisse, Henri 16, 93
mental illness 102, 115
Michelangelo 9; Sistine
    Chapel 41
Monroe, Marilyn 114
Moore, G. E.: intuitionism 19;
    naturalistic fallacy 19;
    Principia Ethica 19–20
morality 20, 54, 95, 125
Morris, William 41–2
music 13, 25

naturalistic fallacy 19
neo-Wittgensteinians 71,
    108
Newman 76
Nicholson, Ben 103–5
novel, the 80, 81

open and closed concepts
    72–3
Osmonds, The **64**, 69

Pacheco, Ana Maria 48-9
passport photographs **44**,
    117
philosophy and art 2–3, 5
photography **44**, **64**, 105–8,
    120, 127–33, **128**
Picasso, Pablo 4, 16, 41
Piero della Francesca 21,
    22
planning 40–4
Plato 29, 66
poetry 42–3
Pollock, Jackson 76;
    Summertime 94
pop art 90

portraits 27–32, **28**, **30–1**, **44**, **64**, 117
Post-Impressionism 15–16, 18; London exhibitions (1910, 1912) 9, 22
Postmodernism 128–9
Poussin, Nicolas 21, 22
Prinzhorn, Hans: *The Artistry of the Insane* 102
procedural theory of art 90–1
proprietorial right 113–14
Psycho (film) 52–4, **53**, 61–2
psychotherapy 60

radio 54
Ramsay, Alan: *David Hume* 27, **28**, 117
Rawls, John 33
readymades 2–3, 73, 99, 113, 123
reflective equilibrium 33
religious art 60–1
Rembrandt 77
representation 10–12, 18, 26, 27–9, 33, 76
resemblance 81
Richardson, Samuel 80
ritual 51
Rodin, August: *The Kiss* 65
Rosenberg, Harold 2–3
Rothko, Mark 76
'Rule Britannia' 51
rules 67–8
Ruskin, John 26

Salle, David 107
Santa Sophia 21
Sargent, John Singer 22
Schopenhauer, Arthur 13
seeing 94
Shakespeare, William 54
Shankly, Bill 67
Sheppard, Anne: misreading of Collingwood 42
Sherman, Cindy 112; *Untitled Film Still #21* 122, 127–33, **128**
significant form 5, 22, 37, 83; defined 10, 23–4
Sistine Chapel 41
Society for Independent Artists 2
Socrates 4, 66
status 98, 99, 100, 100–1, 103, 109, 110
Stein, Pat 107
Stieglitz, Alfred 2–3
Storyville 105
Sylvester, David 44–8

technical theory of art 40–4
timelessness 15, 37
Turner Prize 73
Twombly, Cy 107

universality 15, 37
Ur-art 116

Van Gogh, Vincent 94–5; *A Pair of Shoes* **36**, 50–1

Vasari, Giorgio: *The Lives of the Artists* 9
Venice Biennale 1
Vermeer, Jan 77

Wallinger, Mark: *A Real Work of Art* **xii**, 2, 3, 79, 80, 89, 101, 112, 117, 122
Wallis, Alfred 103–5, 112, 114, 115; *Schooner under the Moon* **107**
Warhol, Andy 34; *Brillo Box* 91, **92**, 123
Waugh, Evelyn: *Brideshead Revisited* 12–13
Weitz, Morris: 'The role of theory in aesthetics' 72–3, 74–7, 78–84, 97, 108, 112, 122
Wilkinson, Robert: misreading of Collingwood 43
Wilton Diptych, The **58–9**, 60–1, 112
Wittgenstein, Ludwig 5, 66–7, 121; family resemblance 68, 72, 82, 83–4, 122; games 66–71, 84; *Philosophical Investigations* 68–70
Wolfe, Tom: *The Painted Word* 99–100
Wood, Christopher 103–5
Woolf, Virginia: *To the Lighthouse* 80